The World's Greatest Speakers

THE
WORLD'S GREATEST
SPEAKERS

Insider Secrets on How to Engage
and Move Your Audience to Action

MARIA LYNN JOHNSON

For Dad

TABLE OF CONTENTS

ACKNOWLEDGMENTS

I am extremely grateful to the many people who have provided support and contributed to the creation of this book.

Thank you to my family, my original speech coaches: My father Jim, who left us way too early; my mother Sandra; my stepfather Dan; my sister Lisa; my brother-in-law Michael; my brother Scott; and my sister-in-law Linda. You are my touchstone and my favorite tribe.

To my kids, Parker and Hailey, my raison d'etre. You are my sun, my moon, and remind me daily just what beauty God can bring onto this earth. Thank you for eating pizza for six months.

To my best friend, Judith, who has been my constant companion and support for 25 years. Without you, I wouldn't be the person I am today.

To Kathryn and Fraser Calhoun, the marketing and publishing team that patiently helped me birth this book. Thank you for your guidance and for withstanding my meltdowns.

To my talented editor, Lisa Derr, who helped me shape the book I wanted to write. Thank you for pulling the all-nighters with me.

A special thank you goes out to: Sheryl Bernstein, my dear friend and creativity coach; Roxann Keyes, the angel that showed up at just the right time; Shari Fleming, my amazing photographer; Mrs. Jeri Kimmel, my high school speech teacher; and my ex-husband Stuart, who helped me bring into this world and raise two amazing children.

My humble gratitude and appreciation to: Mike Koenigs, Ed Rush, Michelle Schiller, Tammy Lawman, Susan Scharenbroich, Naomi McKenna, Rocky Gomez, and all my friends and supporters not mentioned here.

And finally, the master speakers who agreed to be interviewed for this book. Thank you for openly and honestly sharing your stories to inspire, teach, and change people's lives.

INTRODUCTION

It was a Friday. I was sitting at a networking event and the leader had just asked everyone to go around the room. "Tell us who you are, what kind of work you do, and what you hope to get out of today." As the introductions began, I studied each person's approach. But, more interesting was observing those people down the line who were waiting their turns. Their eyes were wide staring at each speaker as each one slowly stood up. I knew that look. Not being quite sure of yourself, comparing each person's elevator speech and deciding whether yours will be as good. *Will I look and sound confident? Think! What is a unique way to introduce myself so I sound cool and look like I really know what I'm talking about? Quick. It's almost my turn.* Your mind races as they get closer. Your mouth goes dry as the person next to you finishes, and all heads turn toward you.

Ever been there? Well, I was at that meeting last week and several people there fell into that familiar place of self-doubt. At the end of the event, after hearing my introduction, a few people approached me about their goals in speaking. One woman in particular said, "I'm never comfortable doing these introductions. I find myself watching everyone else and trying to say just the right thing."

If this resonates with you, you're not alone. Most humans are afraid to speak in front a group; we were designed that way. The irony is that every great movement that has advanced humanity has been inspired through speaking.

What if you could get to a place where talking in front of an audience felt natural and energized everyone in the room? If, when speaking, you could see people's faces change as they became inspired and connected to you and your message.

You can find that place, and this book will get you there. You have a gift to share, a 'secret sauce' that only you can deliver. And people are waiting for it. Sharing your gift can inspire new ideas, change lives, and even start movements. And learning to speak authentically from your core will grow your business, change your life, and expand the lives of others around you.

My goal with this book is for you to become inspired by the journeys, lessons, and insights of 20 master speakers and get out there to share your own message. If you're reading this book, then you have a desire to speak, improve and grow. And whether you're new to speaking or have been speaking for a while, the insights captured here will help you become stronger and better at your craft.

I realize you have many things clamoring for your time and attention, so I don't take it lightly that you're here. To be sure you're spending your time wisely, check out if any of these resonate with you.

This book is for you if:

- You'd rather get a root canal than stand up in front of others and speak, but you know you need to for your business or career to grow.
- You sometimes feel like a fraud or that you have to "fake it" when you speak.
- You've seen speakers and thought, "Hey, I could be doing that! (or doing it even better!)"
- You sometimes question your value, "Who am I to stand up and be the expert?"
- You're overwhelmed and don't know where to start.
- You aren't clear on your message and not sure how to get to that core, genuine place.
- You're afraid that you'll forget your talk and look like an idiot.

- You've been speaking and need to uplevel your skills and approach.

- You have all the confidence in the world, but just need the insights, techniques and direction to guide you as you build your business and speaking career.

If any of these ring true for you, know that you're not alone, so go easy on yourself. By reading this book, you're already on the path to becoming a confident, powerful speaker. In each chapter, successful speakers guide you to understand the core elements of great speaking. They share how they got to where they are, the difficulties along the way, and how they got past each hurdle. They will shift your mindset to what is possible for you and your audiences as you share your unique and important voice with the world.

Each chapter contains an informative and heartfelt interview with a speaker who has made the journey and changed thousands, even millions of lives. I've selected speakers with a variety of backgrounds and perspectives including keynote, platform, selling from the stage, corporate training, workshops, television, and virtual speaking. The interviews are self-contained and can be read in any order, so feel free to jump around.

I am blessed to have had the opportunity to connect with every one of these amazing people, and was fascinated by the common themes that emerged including:

- The difficulty of revealing yourself and becoming vulnerable so you can truly connect with your audience

- The mindset you need to have as you prepare and begin your talk

- The dedication, commitment, and work it takes over time to hone your craft

- The mistakes and lessons learned along the way that are part of the journey

▸ The process of overcoming fear by getting out of your own head and remembering that you're there to serve

▸ The variety of entry points available into public speaking and what you need to do to build a viable business and speaking practice

Many of the speakers have contributed gifts for you, the reader, and each chapter contains instructions on how to access and learn more about the speaker. To get the most out of this book, continue asking yourself, "How does this apply to me?" I also recommend taking notes as you read to capture ideas and plan your next actions around them. Write in it, highlight your favorite sections, and revisit them often. Then put your ideas into action. I hope you see this as an exciting beginning or upleveling of your purpose-driven and profitable speaking career and invite you to join us, lean in and enjoy the conversation.

BE SURE TO ACCESS YOUR FREE BONUS PAGE! YOU'LL RECEIVE:

1) A practical QUICK START SPEAKING GUIDE with steps to get ready and booked

2) A powerful ANTHOLOGY OF QUOTES from the speakers

3) Exclusive access to my weekly SPEAKER NOTES, which include relevant, cutting edge tips and techniques on the concepts covered in the book. You'll also receive the inside scoop on what's happening with me and the speakers in this book.

Get it all NOW at: www.MariaLynnJohnson.com/bonus

CHAPTER 1:
BRIAN TRACY

"After all the money and everything else is gone, the only thing that you'll remember is the shine or sparkle in the face of the listener."
-Brian Tracy

 Brian Tracy is Chairman and CEO of Brian Tracy International. He is among the top speakers, trainers, coaches and seminar leaders in the world today. Brian has consulted for more than 1,000 companies and addressed more than 5,000,000 people in 5,000 talks and seminars throughout the U.S., Canada and 76 other countries worldwide. As a popular keynote speaker and seminar leader, he addresses more than 250,000 people each year. Brian is the top selling author of 80 books that have been translated into 42 languages. He's written and produced more than 300 audio and video learning programs, including the worldwide, best-selling Psychology of Achievement, which has been translated into 28 languages.

Welcome, and thank you for being here, Brian!

Hello, Maria. How are you?

I'm terrific. It's a pleasure talking with you. You've been a leader and a pioneer in the speaking industry for decades, but paint a picture for us. How did it all start?

What we do in life is mostly for survival. I worked at laboring jobs, but when I couldn't get a laboring job, I got a sales job. I learned how to sell well because I studied the heck out of selling. I read everything I could find and worked 10, 12, even 14 hours a day knocking on doors. And of course, speaking is selling. All of speaking is basically an attempt to convey your beliefs to the other person and have them accept those beliefs. If they do, you are successful as a speaker, and if they don't, you are not.

How did you move from sales into training and speaking?

I became successful as a sales person and then the company said, "Why don't you recruit some people and train them on what you're doing?" I did and I put together a sales presentation, a sales formula. I began to teach people how to sell from beginning to end, step-by-step. I have found that there is success formula for every activity in life. Just like a recipe that has a certain number of ingredients. If you mix it in a proper order, in proper proportion, and in the proper way, you will become better. Then you keep improving on the formula. I became successful at sales and then I began to teach people how to sell, which is speaking. I continued training larger groups, so I had to do more preparation. From the beginning to the end, preparation is 80 or 90 percent of your success. If you do the right preparation then almost everything else will flow. If for any reason you neglect the preparation, it will come back to bite you.

What's the worst thing that has happened to you as a speaker and how did you recover?

I remember many years ago, I'd given the same talk several times and I had prepared it very carefully each time. I would review it from beginning to end. One day, I remember, I got so confident that I thought, "I don't need to prepare tonight. I've given it so many times. Who is going to know? I know far more than they do about the subject. No need to prepare." I still remember, I got up there without having prepared and I began to speak. Within about 10 or 15 minutes, I felt like the wheels were coming off my car. I was unsure of where I was. I was making mistakes. I was doubling back on my tracks and saying, "Oh, did I mention this? Let me mention this." "You've said that already." "Oh, did I say this?" "No, you didn't." "Okay." It went back and forth and I just felt mortified, so I made a decision. I still remember the time, the place, the date, the hotel, the room. I made a decision I would never ever again speak without reviewing every single detail thoroughly in advance, even if I've given the talk a hundred times. One of the most important things a speaker can ever learn is that there is no such thing as, "over prepared."

You have so much experience and insight now. What was it like when you started out?

When I started off, I lived in a small room, had old clothes, and was broke most of the time. I didn't know any of this. I learned everything from scratch. I did hundreds of hours of research, training, going to seminars, reading books and taking notes, to develop my first seminar. I would tell my own story but only to illustrate my key points. When I speak, people realize that it's not about me, it's about them. It's always 'you' [the audience]. We are always talking about you. "Have *you* ever had this experience? Have *you* ever done this?"

That's a great perspective.

Oh, it's so important. You have to love the people in your audience and you have to want to help them. For example, I would always open with an upbeat comment so you build expectations right out of the gate. Begin by saying, "This is a wonderful time to be alive." Sometimes, I've been speaking when it has been a disaster in the economy, and sometimes, when it's been a boom. I'll say, "We're going through 'blank' type of economy. The good news is that more people are going to earn more money in this field in the years ahead than has ever been earned in all of human history. Your job is to be one of them and my job is to help you to get there. Would that be a good use of our time today?"

Oh, I love it.

They just love it. They nod and they smile. I learned this by hiring the best speaking coach in the world for ten years. I would bring him to my seminars and have him sit at the front and take notes. Then he would walk through each part and say to me, "Say it like this and do it like that." "It's not as good as it could be," and he would roll it back. It's the most amazing thing. I was giving a 20-minute keynote talk to about a thousand people. I approached him and said, "I want to give you this 20-minute talk and then I want you to critique it." I would give the first sentence of the talk and he would give the timeout sign, "Stop. Repeat that sentence again but only this time, put emphasis on the second word rather than the first word." I would say, "Okay." I would repeat it again and try to get to the next sentence and he would say, "No, no, no. Slow down and put the emphasis on this phrase." He would do this over and over and sometimes, he would keep me repeating a particular sentence, phrase, paragraph for three hours. I said, "But I want to really polish my whole talk." He said, "No, what you do is, deliver one line beautifully so it runs just like music. Then it iterates and every other line that you do within that talk will follow the same musical scale." That just blew me away.

What an interesting, creative approach.

Oh, yeah. I realize that it's better to say far less, say it slowly, and deliver it from your heart than it is to speak really fast. I learned that the most impactful element in a speech is silence. It's the pause and silence. I would say, "How many people here would like to double their income in the next six to 12 months?" Pause, stop. Never ask a question without giving people a chance to take the question and turn it over in their mind like looking at a lovely piece of jewelry and turning it over and studying it. Just pause and smile, like you're talking to your best friend. Then they nod and smile and raise their hands and so on. Then say, "Well, if I could give you some techniques that are used by the highest paid sales people in every industry that are guaranteed to work, for everybody, everywhere, would you give them a try?" Everybody says, "Yeah. I would do that. I would try them out." They nod to each other. I'd say, "Good. I promise you this. I am going to give you at least three proven techniques today that will enable you to double your income in as little as seven days. I know they work because I've taught them to people all over the world and it works for everybody. Would that be a good use of our time?" They all nod and smile, then I deliver.

I love how you lay out such a powerful goal. Who can resist that?

Yes, but you never promise something without delivering on it. And you go slowly, sort of like directing an orchestra. You ask the question and then you go silent and wait. One of the things I learned from my coach, Ron Arden, is that everything is about the pause in speaking. Music has seven notes. [singing] *Do, ti, la, so, fa, me, re, do*. All music has pauses between the notes. Is it a long pause, a short pause or an extended pause? All music is shaped by the pauses between the notes and it's the same thing with speaking.

Some people who are in a service-oriented business shy away from the concept of selling. What would you say to them?

The most important thing is persuasion. Daniel Pink wrote a book called, *To Sell is Human*. He said, "47% of people's job is to move people." He doesn't call it selling, he calls it "moving." It's getting people to move from where they are today in thinking and actions, to where you want them to go. Whether it is to buy a product, accept an idea, or complete a job well. Whatever it is. You are always moving people to take actions differently than they would have in the absence of your influence.

It's all about influence.

Yes, but influence is another word for selling. Many people say, "I'm not a good sales person." My response is, "Everyone sells, the only difference is that some people are good at it and some people are not. Those who are not say, 'I don't like selling'." But, even when you are driving in traffic and you want to change lanes and the person ahead of you has got the lane and you start waving your hand and making signals and pointing to where you want to go, you are engaging in active selling and persuasion to get them to pull back or move forward to let you in. All of life is selling.

What advice do you have for people getting into speaking?

You should speak about something you really care about. Then ask, why do you want to speak well? What is your goal? What is your purpose? You also need to decide what kind of speaking you want to do. Do you want to do keynotes, seminars, workshops, motivational, or business speaking? Many people say, "I want to be a keynote speaker." I say, "Really? Have you done any keynote speaking?" "No. I've seen a lot of people do it, it looks easy." I say, "Keynote speaking is one of the most difficult things in the entire world to do because it is compressing and condensing every single thing that you need to do to be successful in 20 or 30 minutes." Whatever you decide, it has to be something you are passionate about. Fortunately, I backed into this. I thought that people could be far more successful and happy in life if they knew some of these concepts. You will only be successful speaking if you are speaking about something that you care about.

How does that improve your speaking?

Because successful speaking is below the radar level. You affect people at an emotional level because you are talking about something you really care about. If you care about it then *they* start to care about it. You can even start speaking about something that the audience doesn't care about yet, but as you talk about it, they become more and more excited about the subject. I don't know if you ever saw the movie about Johnny Cash with Reese Witherspoon, Walk the Line?

Yes.

At one point, Sam Goody said to Johnny Cash, "If you were hit by a car and you were lying there and realized you were going to die…these are the last few moments of your life and you could only say one message. What one message would you want to convey to the people gathered around you? What are the last words you would want to say?" I say this to my speaking clients. When people want to learn how to speak well, you need to have a message that is so powerful and resonates so strong with you that if you could only give one message, this would be the one that you give. Then that's what you convey. You build on this like a bull's eye on a target that has all the circles around it. Bigger and bigger. Everything starts from there.

Brian, I talk to many people and ask, who do you admire as a speaker? Many times your name comes up. I'm curious, who does Brian Tracy look up to and admire as a speaker?

There's never been just one. Every successful speaker is good at something. I've combined and used things from many speakers. I attended all the seminars given by people like Zig Ziglar back in the day, Denis Waitley and Jim Rohn, the motivational speakers. To me, the only thing that ever matters is to get up and apply the material I learn right now. I have listened to hundreds of speakers and audio programs.

And after all that, what would you say is one of the keys to successful speaking?

The key to successful speaking is to build a bridge with the audience. Connect as quickly as possible so that you can begin talking about something that is important to them and you. I've seen many speakers come and go. Many who were the top speakers in the country are gone. They started off speaking because they felt they had a message that could really help people, but they fell in love with themselves as the speaker. They kept telling their story and talking about themselves. Pretty soon, people didn't want to hear anymore. And the promoters didn't want to promote it. Remember this. It's not about you. It's about them.

I listened to your cassette tapes for years beginning in my 20s, and I know many others did, as well. What does it feel like to have been such an influential and intimate part of so many people's lives?

Well, thank you very much for asking but it never really occurred to me. You and I want to make a difference in the lives of other people. After all the money and everything else is gone, the only thing that you'll really remember is the shine or sparkle in the face of the listener. Someone listened to you and nodded and smiled, and you could see especially when they nudge the person next to them, or they turn and look at the person next to them and then come back. That stays with you for life, whereas what they pay you for tonight and tomorrow is something else. You'll forget that by the end of the week. The great joy of this comes from a positive effect on others in some way.

How did you come up with The Psychology of Achievement?

I went to a seminar decades ago and the person who gave the seminar was talking about the importance of self-esteem. He said, how you feel about yourself determines how you feel about other people. How you feel about them determines how you treat them and how they treat you right back. I'd never heard that before. Your level of self-esteem, how much you like yourself determines how much you like others and how much they like you back and how successful and happy they'll be. I thought, "Wow. Good grief." It's about the words you use, like simply saying, "I like myself," over and over again. "I like myself, I like myself." I started off by giving a seminar called, "The Phoenix Seminar: The Psychology of Achievement." People would listen to the seminar, come up and say, "You profoundly changed my life." They listen to the seminar and they begin to apply the principles which are all based around self-esteem, self-responsibility, self-reliance, and self-goals. Every part of their lives improves, their families, their sales and their self-esteem. I have hundreds of thousands of people who have written to me, who have come up to me in seminars and say, "Those words, 'I like myself' changed my life forever."

I can remember when my brother was raising his first child. He taught her to say that. She was just a little peanut and she would walk around saying, "I like myself, I like myself." Eventually all of his kids learned it.

Isn't that wonderful? By the way, my first daughter was Christina. They called her peanut. I raised all my children to have high self-esteem. They really like themselves, they love themselves. You can see it because they shine. Anyway, that's how I began speaking with a subject that I love to do.

And how did that lead into, "The Psychology of Selling?"

Event planners would say, "We realize this is a motivational seminar, but we want to just cut straight to the chase. We want you to get to the seminar that's just about sales. Straight to sales, right now." Eventually, I adjusted the seminar and developed the program called, The Psychology of Selling. More people have become millionaires by listening to the Psychology of Selling than any other influence in their lives. But, what they tell me when I see them is, "You've changed my life profoundly. It helped me make a lot of money, but more important it changed my personality, my relationship with my spouse and my children. It raised my self-confidence and self-esteem, made me like myself and respect myself. As a result, it iterated into sales, like dominoes that just go click, click, click. Because I like myself so much, I like my customers. Because I like my customers, my customers like me and because they like me, they bought from me. Then they recommend me to their friends." Quite astonishing.

In all those years then as a writer, speaker, thought leader. What has surprised you the most?

Many people have the idea that they are largely fixed so their level of thoughts, feelings, emotions, background history, is kind of locked in. It's not changeable. I began to study, and I combined the whole idea of self-esteem with the development of human potential. I've found that the greatest obstacle to success is negative emotions. Negative emotions stand in the way and block you. We can eliminate negative emotions and then all that's left is positive emotions. The reason people have low self-esteem is because they are negative about themselves and their potential. I began to explain the importance of high self-esteem and the importance of eliminating negative emotions. What I found was that you can transform yourself, you can become a completely positive person by feeding yourself with new information. I began to do this and put together messages that enable other people to do it and it has been transforming for millions of people.

How did this shape your speaking?

I started off speaking at the age of 36. You can't just start off speaking like my friend Bill Gove. We all agreed that Bill Gove was probably the best speaker in America and people would come up to Bill at the National Speakers Association and say, "I want to be a good speaker like you." He would say, "Why? Why do you want to be a speaker?" Bill said, "It's not enough to want to make a lot of money. It's got to be something bigger than that. It's okay to be financially successful and highly respected and get standing ovations, but it has to help other people. It has to have an effect that changes their lives forever." What makes me happy is when people come up and say, "I read your book, No Excuses: The Power of Self-Discipline," and they smile. They act as though they just found gold. "It is such a great book." It made them so happy to get the message.

Walk me through the structure of a talk. How do you begin?

First, what do you want to speak about? You must be crystal clear about what you are going to say. The opening is to get their attention and settle them down. For example, "How many people here would like to double their income? You are sales people in a busy sales world," you've got everybody's attention. Everybody is there.

What comes next?

The introduction. The introduction is the reason for being there in the first place. I always explain two things. The problem that will be solved, and the goal that will be achieved. The worst thing that can happen in a speech is when people don't know why they are there. That must be crystal clear. Have you ever sat next to somebody, and I've had a friend actually lean over and say, where is he going with this? A really good talk has clear goals, so everybody knows that every single word is aimed at those goals. Then you bridge from there into what I call MOS, My Own Story.

What does that look like?

MOS is a personal, signature story that you share about how this relates to you. "I started poor, I had no money, I had no friends, I had no skills," and so on. It has to have changed your life in some way, it contains a lesson or moral for others, and you were not the same person afterwards. When you tell your story, it needs to generate emotion in you and the audience. It's really the core or heart of your talk. It takes time to polish this and make it relevant.

Once you're in the talk, how do you recommend people tell stories?

Well, once you tell your own story, you move into your content, which has three main points. When you tell a story it has to relate to a point you're making. I've seen some of the most successful speakers in the world tell a story that has nothing to do with the subject. I remember a top speaker told this story and everybody laughed. Afterwards, I said, "Tell me, why did you tell that story? It doesn't have anything to do with anything." He said, "Yeah, but it's entertaining and people like to be entertained." And I'm just shaking my head. I never say a word that is not tied in to something, that does not coordinate with the message, and that does not somehow help the person achieve the goal or solve the problem."

What's the best way to develop a story?

Developing a story is like shifting gears, and you always begin with a transition. This could be, "Once upon a time…" "That reminds me of a story." "Did you ever hear about…?" When you tell the story, it should have a logical development. And, as you close the story, it should end with an unexpected twist that makes a key point.

Are there some key principles people should follow around delivering a story?

First, it must be short and to the point, and illustrate a good idea. You should bridge off the story to the point you are trying to make. You want to make people think or laugh, but you're not telling a story just to entertain. I won't use humor often. I used to get kicked out of school when I was young, kicked out of classes. They sent me to the library and I spent many, many hours there because I was a troublemaker. I would read the joke books, that was my form of entertainment. I tell jokes only when it illustrates a key point. If it doesn't hook into something, then don't tell it.

What are things you can do to get your audience to like you?

That's persuading and influencing your audience. Remember, every speech has a job to do. The ultimate goal is that people take action they otherwise wouldn't have taken. There's a thing called the 'likeability factor'. Here, we call it the 'friendship factor'. What it basically says is, "If people really like you, you can say anything and you'll be successful. If people don't like you, you can be a brilliant speaker and nothing will happen." You build this by treating them as though you're friends, smiling and treating them warmly.

What are some techniques to do this?

Take the time to determine what they want, need or hope for. I called this the 'hopes and dreams factor' because when you talk to people about their hopes and dreams, and what they should do to improve their lives, then they lean forward and listen very closely. Take the time to determine what they want. Identify the gap between where they are now and where they could be if they followed your advice. Use words like "imagine," to get them to "see" how what you teach could be of advantage to them. This is your homework. Before you stand up and speak to them, make sure that you know who they are and what they want, the problems and difficulties that they're facing, and how you can help them achieve that.

Can you give an example of what this would sound like?

A simple one is to say that the market has turned down dramatically recently. "Sales in this industry are down 33%, and your sales are down 27%, even though you have a great product. It's superior to almost anything else that's out there, isn't that true?" Everybody nods. "You have to turn that around, don't you?" "Yes, we do." "I'm about to give you some ideas to sell higher price products against lower price products. You create products at a higher price than your competitors, isn't that true?" "Yes. We're always saying, 'Well, it cost too much. I can get it cheaper somewhere else.'" "Yes. Well, I am going to show you how price is not a factor when a customer comes to buying your product or service, and I'll show you how to counter balance price against quality and how you can show them that buying your product at a higher price is the smartest thing they can do." They're taking notes. I haven't even told them anything yet, but I'm promising to help them fulfill their hopes and dreams. That's why it helps to determine the goals and ambitions of the people you're talking to in advance.

This is where you check in with the meeting planner.

It's very important to go in prepared. You need to ask every question you possibly can to learn what your audience is thinking and feeling, and what they're consumed about and worried about. Then, focus on helping them solve their problems, and achieve their goals. Do your homework, learn everything you can about the audience in advance to speaking to them. Nothing is more impressive.

Is there anything you can say that applies to most audiences?

Here's stuff that I always say, "I understand that you are among the top sales people in this industry worldwide. Is that true?" Never get disagreement. I say, "I'm going to talk to you as some of the top people in this industry and give you ideas that you can use immediately to get better results than you have ever done before. Would that be a good use of our time?" "Absolutely." "Good." Always talk to them as if they are superior. Here's an interesting thing. Many people talk to their audiences as if the audience is a little bit deficient and they've come along to help them. Always talk to your audience as if they are outstanding, and it's quite amazing. Some speakers stand up and ask if you're worried about business, you don't have enough money, your bills are too high, and so on. It's all the negatives in life. I've never done that in my whole career. I always talk about the positive, how good they are, how good the company is, and how good the industry is. Always build them up. Always make them feel happier and more valuable.

Those are great tips, thank you. Brian, if you could have dinner with anyone, living or not living, who would that be?

I would say, it would be somebody like Winston Churchill. Another is a man named Ludwig von Mises. Ludwig von Mises was an Austrian economist who began writing early in the century. He was one of the most brilliant thinkers, and changed the direction of almost the entire country. There have been two or three Nobel prize winners who are direct descendants of Ludwig von Mises.

My final question is piggy-backing on the story you told earlier about the movie. You are at the last moments of your life. You can say one thing, what would be the most meaningful thing you'd want to say?

Well, I started to think about this 20-25 years ago as I went for a long walk on the beach in Brisbane, Australia. I said to myself, "What would I like to accomplish in my life?" I said, "I would like people to say that I was a great person." I said, "What does that mean?" The answer was that my children would say, "My father was a great father." I thought about that, I walked for miles, I am walking the whole afternoon. "What would I have to do? How would I have to live, treat them, and behave for them to say that?" I organized my whole life around that and never changed it. I've always behaved so that at the end of the day, people would say, "He was a great father. He was a great husband."

That's wonderful. My goal with this information and the book is to inspire people to embrace their own voice, get out there, share their message, and change the world. And you've helped do just that.

I've so enjoyed connecting with you, Brian.

Thank you, Maria. Good luck with the book.

KEY TAKEAWAYS

‣ Speaking is selling.

‣ Preparation is 80 to 90 percent of your success.

‣ Love the people in your audience.

‣ Ask a question, then pause and wait.

‣ Speak on something you're passionate about.

ABOUT BRIAN TRACY

Brian speaks to corporate and public audiences on Personal and Professional Development, including the executives and staff of many of America's and the world's largest corporations. Prior to founding Brian Tracy International, Brian was the Chief Operating Officer of a $265 million development company. He has conducted high level consulting assignments with several billion-dollar corporations on strategic planning and organizational development. He has traveled and worked in over 120 countries on six continents and speaks four languages.

CONTACT

You can learn more about Brian by visiting his website www.BrianTracy.com, where you can download his free 12-step Goal-Setting Guide, as well as visit his page of Free Resources. He is available on social media.

CHAPTER 2:
SUZE ORMAN

"Nerves are just a precursor to greatness, if you're willing to face them."
-Suze Orman

Suze Orman has been called "a force in the world of personal finance" and a "one-woman financial advice powerhouse" by *USA Today*. She is one of the best-selling authors of all time having written 9 consecutive New York Times bestsellers with over 30 million copies of her books in print all over the world. A two-time Emmy Award winner, Suze was the host of the *Suze Orman Show*, which aired worldwide on CNBC for 14 years. Business Week named Suze one of the top ten motivational speakers in the world. She was the only woman on that list, making her 2007's top female motivational speaker in the world. Suze was named by Forbes as one of "The World's 100 Most Powerful Women." Twice *Time Magazine* named her as one of the TIME 100, the World's Most Influential People.

Welcome, and thank you so much for being here today, Suze.

You're welcome, Maria.

How did you begin speaking and what was that growth journey like?

In the early 80s, I was working at Merrill Lynch as a broker. Pacific Gas and Electric, which is the utility company from Northern California, was having retirement seminars. None of the experienced brokers at Merrill Lynch wanted to give those seminars because nobody ever retired from Pacific Gas and Electric. You weren't paid to give those seminars. You just gave them in the hopes that one day you would get clients. I was still brand new, so I said, "I'll do it." I started to speak in front of the five people who would come. Then, a few months later, they asked me to come back, and it was 10 people. Before you knew it, they were asking me to come back all the time and I was speaking to 50 people. I was giving the same talk over and over again, educating them on their retirement benefits. The more I gave the same talk, the more I was able to do it without notes.

What happened after Merrill Lynch?

I eventually started my own firm, The Suze Orman Financial Group. Sure enough, the people from Pacific Gas and Electric eventually had an early retirement. All of the people came to me, but so many people wanted to hear me speak that I had to do it on film, so tens of thousands could hear me speak little by little. That's how I started to learn how to speak. It was the greatest thing that ever happened to me.

What a great story.

The other thing Maria, is it never dawned on me that anybody would ever pay me to speak. I never spoke to get money. I spoke because I loved the material and the effect it was having on people. That was my reward and that's what kept me going. Too many times people get on the stage, and they're doing it for a paycheck. Their talks are flat and rehearsed. It was never for the money. I was shocked the first time somebody paid me to speak.

You have this strong but loving way of kicking people in the behind to get them to take action and improve their financial situations. Where does that part of you come from?

Part comes from me just being me. Out of all the topics to speak on, the hardest is money. Not just what stock to buy, but personal finance…the moves that every person needs to make with their money. They don't want to hear it and they don't want to do it. They are fine spending hundreds or thousands of dollars to go to a motivational talk, but why are they all doing it? They want to be motivated to go and make money. It's the end result of all of their actions. But it's the one topic they do not want to hear.

What was it like after you started your own firm?

You know, I had more clients than I knew what to do with. When there is a cause of why you're doing what you are doing, not "let me just impart this information to you," but "let me make you independent. Let me help make you strong. Let me help make you the master of your financial destiny," it's not hard to find the passion to speak. I'm not conveying ideas. I'm conveying truths that will change your life. Everybody feels like I am speaking directly to them because I am. Because every single person, no matter what race, religion, sexual preference, tax bracket, or what they are, relates to money in the exact same way.

Since this was something they didn't want to hear about or talk about, did you find resistance in the audience?

No. Somehow, everybody resonated with the message and my story. They loved that I wasn't one of these people who married into money, or was raised with money. They loved that my English wasn't perfect. They loved that I said things that "normal" financial advisors would never say. There was an exchange of values between me and the audience, and somehow they resonated with those values. It was an amazing thing to see.

What was it like when your practice grew and your message was spreading?

It was difficult when I first went to South Africa and China, because I didn't know if this message would translate all over the world, but it did. The message wasn't, "Do this with your money. Do that with your money." It was a message of, "Why don't you do that which you know you should do with money? Why are you being an obstacle in your own path to financial freedom? You can be the master of your financial destiny. Who you are directly affects what you make and how much you get to keep."

It's not about the numbers, it's really about your mindset and your beliefs.

Fear, shame, and anger are the internal obstacles to wealth. Money is a physical manifestation of who you are. It was a broader definition and these were ideas that they had never heard before. There were no books that talked about that before. Behavioral economics stem from my work, not the other way around. And the men liked it as much as the women. The acceptance from the press wasn't immediate, but the acceptance from the talks was immediate.

What was the worst experience you've had speaking?

One time I went to Canada to speak and I did not like it. A good speaker should feel better when he or she has left the stage than before they entered the stage. And even though I got a standing ovation from five thousand people, I have never been back to Canada to speak again. During the entire talk, they didn't react or give me feedback. They were so polite and such great people, that they sat and waited until they were supposed to applaud. For me, it was the most miserable talk of my life.

That sounds rough.

I couldn't feel them. And I couldn't feel them because they weren't allowing themselves to feel and react when there should have been a reaction, you know. It was miserable and I didn't care that I got great reviews. A speaker has to love every moment that they're on that stage. When they walk off that stage, they have to feel that they hit it out of the ballpark and that they loved what they just did because it's that energy that carries them to the next talk.

It's about getting feedback, but it also sounds like it's about getting in front of the right audience.

It is about getting in front of the right audience. I do not like to speak to people with a lot of money, and I consistently turn them down because that is not the right audience for me, wealthy people. And God bless every single one of them.

Why is that?

They can do anything that they want. They can get the best financial advisors. It's the people who don't have a pot to pee in, have credit card debt, have lost their jobs or homes, don't know how to pay their bills, and don't know who to trust. What financial advisor wants to deal with them if all they have is credit card debt? They can't make a commission off them, so those people have nobody to go to. Those are my people. That's who I want. I want 90% of the population.

You're really on a mission. You started a movement a while ago and it has come a long way.

Yes, it has.

When you started speaking to bigger audiences, how did your life change and how did you stay grounded?

I never had to stay grounded because I never related to what was happening. You know, I never saw myself as the world's personal finance expert. I never saw myself as an Emmy award winner. I always saw myself as Suze, and for whatever reason, it just never took over. If you were to interview my staff when I had the TV show, there was never a hierarchy. I was never "the boss." People are people and they have to be valued that way. I would be in public and everybody would come up to me and they'd say, "We love you, Suze," and they would want a hug or autograph. I would do it, but as soon as that moment was over, I went back to just being Suze, as if it had never happened.

Who inspired you? Were there leaders or speakers that you admired as you grew through this?

When I was younger and a financial advisor, I always listened to Bob Brinker, who was on KGO radio back in San Francisco. All these people would come, like Jim Jorgeson, and I would go watch them speak. I was always in awe of them thinking, "Wow, look at all these people who have come to see them speak."

Now here you are, all these years later, with people coming to see you speak.

None of my success was planned. I simply wrote my first book to give to my client to impress them. I thought it was crazy somebody paid me $10,000 to write a book and they were going to give me 50 copies to give to clients for free. There are people who say, "Write down your goals. Be very specific. Imagine what you want and what you will become." Listen, Maria, there is no way possible I could have dreamt or planned the level of success that has been obtained over these years. I didn't even know how to think like that.

Interesting.

It just happened by a lot of hard work. I spent ten years not spending more than two days in one place.

I never said "No." You know, I did 70,000 miles in the month of March in 1998 on a plane on coach, flying back and forth, east coast to west coast and back. I went for it with everything I had, and I didn't have time to stop and think about what was happening.

Which is probably why you were so successful. You know, your mission was to get out there and help people and that's all you thought about.

That's right, that was it. Now I look back and say, "Are you kidding me, Suze Orman?" I'll never forget looking at that USA Today little graph, showing "9 Steps to Financial Freedom" versus all the other books. I loved being on Oprah, but even the Oprah producers will tell you Oprah wanted me on once a week. I said, "I'm not going on once a week. Are you kidding? People will hate us. You can't talk about money to people once a week. They won't like that, Oprah, they'll hate you."

You really knew your audience and how they would respond.

To be a good speaker, you better be in tune with your audience. I don't plan a talk, right? I'm an unscripted talent. Before every single talk, I go through the audience and ask people why they came. What do they need to hear? I will ask everybody until I have a feeling of who they are, and then I give them the talk they need to hear. Not the talk I want to give them. The talk they need to hear, which is the talk I want to give them.

Many people talk about speakers coming out and really grabbing their audience by starting with a powerful question or statement. Your talks are a little different with an educational piece.

Yes, but the educational piece never comes till after the personal piece. Until there's some interaction with me. And to this day, people love to hear my story. You know, I'll ask them, "Have you not heard this story enough, people?" And they say, "Tell it again, Suze." Right? A lot of times I'll open by asking them to please stand up if they have credit card debt, car loan debt, or other bad debt, and the whole audience ends up standing. I look at them and say, "I can't talk to you about money. You don't have any." I ask them to always tell the person next to them how much debt they have. Right there, something has happened in their lives that they've never done before. They've told the truth about their finances to a stranger.

Is that how you always open?

I never know what my talk is going to open with. I have no idea what I'm going to do or not do. None. For me, a talk is nerve-wracking for the first five minutes. Until I've found my footing.

Really?

Oh, of course. I don't have a clue what I'm going to say.

So how do you keep centered and manage your nerves when you're going through that?

I'm like a little racehorse. I literally start thinking, "Let me out there and let me just do it. Don't keep me. Let me go. Let me go. Come on." And everybody around me can see it. I can hear KT (my manager) saying, "She wants to go. Look at her. She's ready to go. Don't keep her much longer. Let her out." My PBS special is the same. Those aren't planned. I walk on stage and there's five cameras and the words come out and it's done. Over.

Well, you know you're being authentic each time if you don't have it planned.

But it is nerve-wracking.

Many people think you have to get rid of that feeling. If you've got a lot of energy going sometimes that's a good sign.

I've always said the day that I'm not nervous or the day there isn't that type of thought, that will probably be the last time I give a good talk. You need that to be able to carry a large audience, and really, a thousand people, when you're looking at them, is a lot. It doesn't look a whole lot different from one thousand to five thousand. And 50,000 doesn't look a whole lot different than 200,000 so it's interesting. You need energy to carry a talk like that. The microphone isn't going to do it. You have to do it. And you have to move.

Tell me about that. How do you use the space?

I never hide. If you've seen my PBS special, you see me standing. I never sit in a chair when giving a talk, and I'm never behind a podium because it blocks your energy. You have to have enough faith in what you're talking about that you don't need any props. I never speak to a slide show. The only thing I do is come out mic'd, and I don't like it when I have to hand hold the mic. I like it when it's on my lapel so I can be animated. You need to be able to move from one end of the stage to the other, but not nervously because they'll get seasick if you move too much.

Sure.

You need to be vulnerable, without hiding behind something so that your audience can become naked with you.

How does someone do that? What advice would you have for people who are having trouble getting there?

I would say, please never think that you're going to speak to a crowd. You're going to speak with people. You're going to have a conversation with them, and if you have to think about what you're going to say before you say it, then it's not a conversation. I don't know the words I'm going to say until they're coming out right here and now. Know what I mean?

Yes.

You have to converse with them and you have to believe that you have something within you that you want them to know because it will help make their lives better. You want that for them. And you want that for yourself, and if that's what you really want, how else can you be but vulnerable and honest and real? Otherwise you're just a stage actor.

Right.

Right?

After all these years and all the talks, what has surprised you the most?

What has surprised me the most? The fact that the times I've been the most nervous are the times that I give the absolute best talks.

It's interesting. Last July, I spoke in front of five thousand women and I hadn't spoken for a long time. To change my personal life, I took a year off. I wanted one year for just me. So, I hadn't spoken for a long time. Here was 5,000 women I was speaking to at Avon. They had just brought on a new CEO and for some reason, I was more anxious about this talk than any talk I'd ever given. I have to tell you I blew it out of the water like nothing ever before.

That's awesome.

Even at the end with the CEO of Avon going, "Woah, what happened there?" That surprised me the most. Once again it taught me that nerves are just a precursor to greatness, if you're willing to face them. I will say one other thing. It is far harder to give a 20-minute talk than it is an hour and a half talk, or a five-minute talk than it is to give a longer talk.

Yeah, you've got to get to the point.

It is very difficult to give a short talk.

Suze, if you could have dinner with anyone, living or not living, who would that be?

Nobody. I don't like eating with people. I'm not kidding. I've never had a business meal or a business dinner.

Okay, how about if you could just sit on your couch just talking with someone?

You know, it's interesting that in my life I've talked to all the people that I've ever wanted to talk to. You know, from Nelson Mandela to Maya Angelou to royalty to presidents to actors to comedians, to all of them. If I could speak right now with one person and be with them again, it would be my dad because my dad died before he saw his little girl turn into the powerhouse that was able to take care of not only herself but my mother, as well. He never thought we would have enough money to be okay. He died at 71, way back in 1981. If I had one person that I could spend time with and talk to and have dinner with, it would be my dad.

Oh, that's so cool. One final question for you. If you knew then what you know now, what would you have done differently?

Nothing. Absolutely nothing.

Interesting.

And the reason is this: everything that's correct and easy and good and successful will never get you to the mature place as a human being you need to be. The negativity, the doubt, the lies and the failures are what make you who you are. Your life is made up of ups and downs, and the key to life is when you can be as happy in your sadness as you are in your happiness. I love everything about my life, who I share my life with, and where I live my life. My life would not be this right now if anything in the past was different, so I don't want anything to change. It's not like I experienced all great stuff. It's the hard stuff and the non-understandable stuff that made me who I am to this day, and I will always thank my parents for poverty. I will always be appreciative of the blame and the shame that came, along with the grace. I would change absolutely nothing.

Find the gift in everything, even the painful stuff. Awesome.

You've got that right, girlfriend.

My goal in this is to inspire people to get their voice out there, and you've done that, so thank you.

Just remember: make it your own voice. Don't let your voice be anybody else's voice. Don't let your tone, the way you speak, the awkward words you may say, or the words you can't pronounce, be anybody else's but yours. Be wary of coaches and people giving advice. Make yourself great, because greatness resides within you, as you. And that's what people want to be touched with. They don't want to be touched with an artificial you.

Suze, it has been such a pleasure talking with you. Thank you for all the great insights. I know a lot of people will get value out of this. I know I did.

There you go, girlfriend. You have a good one, okay?

You too. Thanks, Suze.

KEY TAKEAWAYS:

- Speak because you love the material and the effect it has on people.
- There are no shortcuts, it just takes a lot of hard work.
- You need to be vulnerable so that your audience can become vulnerable *with* you.
- You need energy to carry a large audience.
- Make it your own voice, because greatness resides within you.

ABOUT SUZE ORMAN:

Over her television career, not only is Suze the single most successful fundraiser in the history of PBS, having raised over 200 million dollars with her eight pledge shows, she also has garnered an unprecedented seven Gracie awards, more than anyone in the 42-year history of the award. The Gracies recognize the nation's best radio, television, and cable programming for women. Saturday Night Live spoofed Suze 6 times, and at the age of 30 she was still a waitress making only $400 a month.

CONTACT:

To learn about Suze, you can visit her website at www.suzeorman.com where you'll have access to a free video series. There is a resource center and many how-to videos available, as well as information about Suze's work helping members of the US Military. Suze's active on social media.

CHAPTER 3:
MARK
SCHARENBROICH

"You must have clarity of message, a premise. Where do I want to go, how do I get there and how does this relate to the audience?"
-Mark Scharenbroich

 Mark Scharenbroich ("Sharen-brock") is an award-winning speaker, author, and producer. Today, he and his wife Sue manage Scharenbroich and Associates, a motivational speaking and leadership training video production company. Mark is an award-winning keynote speaker, winner of an Emmy Award as writer/ producer for an ABC TV special, and recipient of several international film awards. In 2003, Mark was inducted into the National Speaker's Association prestigious Hall of Fame. Less than 5% of the professional speakers worldwide have been awarded this honor.

Welcome, and thanks for being here, Mark!

My pleasure, Maria.

Today you're one of the top speakers in the National Speakers Association, but let's back up to newbie Mark. How did you start out and what's your story?

In high school, I started a comedy group with another guy and we started writing and performing our own sketch comedy. There were six of us in the group. We performed in high schools and small colleges doing short sketch comedy. Kind of like Monty Python, pre-Saturday Night Live. When the group broke up, I went back to the same schools we performed in, but doing my own one-man show. In essence, being a motivational speaker for high school students, that was in 1977-78. I was hired by Jostens, the class ring people, as a value-added service for them, to speak at some of their clients' schools. Not about rings or product but about engagement and high school. I was a high school assembly speaker for over 20 years, working gyms across north America. It was an incredible training ground, because it's a tough training ground.

Why is it tough?

You're in a gymnasium, and the sound is questionable. Sometimes it was good, and other times it was terrible, so you had to make it work. The teachers would often be in the hallways or by the gym door so there was no supervision up in the crowd. You had to control the show. Expectations of your audience are extremely low. They're high school students, and they hope you're terrible because it's fun to mock later.

Oh, my gosh.

You had to capture their attention in 30 seconds or less, and take them on an engaging ride. Then support it with a strong message about making healthy choices, being a decent person, and ending with a big finish that would send them on their way just excited. I had to be able to present in a gym without image magnification to 2,000 people, and still be seen by everybody, keep their attention, focus the message, and have it relate to the universal messages. It was great training.

How did you move from that into becoming a professional keynote speaker?

As students grew up, they got jobs in business, and they suddenly had meetings to go to. People would say, "Hey do you know any speakers? We have a conference coming up." Then a previous student would say, "Yeah, I remember a guy back in high school. Let me Google him." As soon as Google came out, people started finding and hiring me. From 2000 until 2005 I transitioned to speaking to associations and business groups. Speaking to those groups is 95% of my work now.

It's interesting that you started out in high schools, and then later the students hired you as a speaker.

You know, supply and demand. There were not that many high school speakers at the time. We were often booked a year in advance. I made a film for Jostens called, "The Greatest Days of Your Life So Far." Meaning that high school's not the best time for everybody, but as long as you're here make these days count. Jostens showed that film during the 1980s in about 10,000 high schools every year for almost ten years. I didn't have any intention of using the film as a marketing tool, but everybody that saw the film said we want the guy live. So bam! That was my big break.

What was it in the way you addressed the audience in the film that drew people to you so much?

The film was about 18 to 20 minutes of me speaking. It was like a Ted Talk, followed by original music and cool scenes of the best moments of high school. We filmed at high schools across the country. But the message was along the lines of my style today. Stories driven with humor with emotional catches and phrases that people remember afterwards.

What do you mean by emotional catches?

My intention is to take people on a bit of an emotional roller coaster ride. The best compliment I can ever receive, is when people come up and say, "Gee, I really liked the talk." And you always ask, "Why? What made it different?" They say, it was like a roller coaster ride. You had me laughing one minute and next to tears in the next." I want to be able to hit universal messages, and touch the heart as much as the funny bone and the head. I also want to have some moments in there that slow it down and allow people to be more reflective. That's hitting all the notes.

I've seen you engage a large audience so well. Like when you conduct the different sections of the audience with your baton.

Yeah, that's a fun piece. I did that for high school students for years. It was my big finish. My talk is about engagement, taking a risk and being involved. So, I thought, here's an activity that's going to pull the whole school together. In essence I'm doing a mime piece, but they're the ones that are actively engaged. My great friend and fellow speaker Erich Chester said, "Why aren't you doing that for adult groups?" I said, "They would never go for it." He said, "How do you know?" So, I tried it out for the first time with a group from Wells Fargo and they liked it better than the high school students did. It was funny. They all turned into sixteen year olds and were cheering for Wells Fargo. So, you never know until you try, right?

What is your process for coming up with the stories?

I watch audiences. I know my material well enough that I'm not guessing what's next. That allows me time to be one with the audience to see what they're doing and how they're reacting. Other speakers talk about the importance of 'blank', and why you should do 'blank', and that's why 'blank' is this. Suddenly you see people looking at their program to see what the next session is, or pouring water into their glass from the pitcher in front of them, or checking their phone. You don't want any of that to be happening. The way around that is a powerful story. As soon as you go into 'once upon a time', the audience members open themselves up to listen to what's next. In my presentations, the lesson is the shortest part of the presentation and it's all story with humor driven to get there. The other thing I do is ad lib the transitions. I know my material, but the transitions I use to get from Story A to Story B? Those are in the moment, those are live. I really don't know what I'm going to say each time.

Do you have something at the end? A call to action?

It all ties in to my core premise, which started back in 2003. I traveled to Neenah, Wisconsin for a presentation, and landed in the middle of a Harley Davidson 100-year anniversary. I'm not a Harley guy at all. I was in a beige rental car. But I'm just taken by these hundreds of thousands of bikers that are in Milwaukee for the week. I pulled over just because it looked so cool and I kept hearing these people walking by each other going, "Oh. Nice bike!" And I saw this connection. The next day I'm talking to teachers in Neenah, helping them kick off the year. I start ad libbing about nice bike. When you're standing by your classroom doorway and kids are coming through the door for the first day of school, instead of saying good morning, you say, "Oh, Maria. I can't believe you're in my class this year, that's so wonderful." That's like nice bike. It's a metaphor about how we connect. The audience members nod. There's a reaction. It's using Maria's name instead of saying, "Hi." That little ad lib. I knew when the audience reacted to it I had something there. I started playing with it and developing it from an ad lib to a short little piece, to a major piece, to my premise and then my whole brand.

How did that impact your talks?

It brought so much more clarity to what I was doing. People would write back, or see me in the hallways and go, "Nice bike." Instead of saying, "Hey, good speech" they'd say, "Nice bike" and I knew that was it. So, how do I end it? Full circle. If you set it up at the end, it will help people remember your message. You're going to be driving down the road and a Harley is going to pass you and when they do, I want you to turn to the person next to you and nice bike them.

How do you go about building your talk around that?

First thing is clarity of message. From beginning, middle to end. What is the premise that's going to carry all the way through? Number two is the content, and there's power in three. I'll come up with three major points to support my premise. My three points are to acknowledge, honor, and connect. I talk about how to make more connections within each of those points. I want you to *acknowledge* them by being present in their lives. I want you to *honor* them by creating a cool experience. I want you to *connect* with them by making that moment personal.

How do you build in stories?

Within those three points I'll have different stories. For example, my presentation is about making meaningful connections. The hook that I have is "nice bike," meaning when you walk up to a Harley person, no matter how tough they look and you go, "Oh! Nice bike." There's this instant connection, smile, and emotion shared. I use that to set up where I want to go. I'm not going to tell a story that doesn't relate. I used to open up with a story about being a hobby parent driving one child, two children or three children. It was a funny opener, but I'd always have a third of the audience looking at me like, where is this going? Are you a comedian? What is this? Then I realized it doesn't support the premise or my three points.

How did you replace your opener?

The documentary by Jerry Seinfeld called "Comedian" is a must view for any performer because there's nobody better in the world than Jerry Seinfeld at the height of the Seinfeld series. There's a great line about taking all your material and throwing it out, and having all the material audition to get back into the show. The documentary opens with him taking all of his great material that he's written over the years and throwing it all into a coffin as his fellow comedians are standing there watching this take place. He goes through the process of starting to work in small clubs, trying out new material and coming up with a new show from scratch. It's a painful process. But, by the end of the year he had a show that was absolutely incredible.

It sounds like you have this process of self-examination and continuous improvement.

Always. I think it should be true of any speaker that if you look at your video from a year ago, two years ago, especially three years ago, you should just cringe. You should think, oh, I do that piece so much better now. Every presentation should be an improvement. I'm fortunate because I'm married to my boss, my director, my co-writer, and my speech coach, Susan. She understands the business and creative side of speaking. What that means is I get an honest appraisal. I've coached a number of speakers. One guy was doing a piece and I said, "You know, I don't like that piece at all." He said, "I really do." I said, "It's too dramatic, you fall onstage. I don't like it." He kept it in and I said, "You know, it's not that I dislike it, I hate it. I hate that thing." He finally dropped it and his wife saw him speak and said, "You didn't do that piece that you always do." He said, "I know. Scharenbroich told me he hated it." And she said, "I hate it, too. I've always hated it." "Why didn't you tell me?" "Well, you're the professional. I thought you knew what you were doing."

That's pretty funny. Some of what you're talking about is accepting that you're going to fall on your face a couple times and that's okay. Because each time you get better.

That's exactly right. I'm a huge fan of the Marx Brothers with all their films back in the Vaudeville days. They would take a show on the road across the country and do about 30 performances or more. Every time they did a show they would tweak a line, deliver it a little bit differently, or try a different shtick until they found the perfect reaction. By the time they did the full run and got to the west coast, they had pushed and tweaked the material so much that it was just perfect. They would make the movie and know exactly where all the laugh lines fall because they'd set it up that way.

How do you apply that to your own work?

Every time I have a story that I like, I change the words around, change the timing, or add a character to it. I don't revamp it entirely, but just make little tweaks here and there. Giving yourself the freedom to play with your material onstage live, allows you to find where the reactions are and what really works. It also keeps you from being so memorized and practiced and perfect. I think any audience would take Velveteen Rabbit over perfect any day.

You really bring your whole self into the experience. How does someone learn to be vulnerable and open up to the audience?

You have to have clarity of message. I know that seems obvious but some speakers kind of wander around and you wonder where they're going with their message. From beginning to middle to end you need a real clear cut, here's where I'm going to go, and here's how I'm going to get there. It gives you the freedom to be more in touch with the audience. It gives you more freedom to be more conversational, which means more authentic, which means not practiced, which means this isn't number 78 of 100 speeches this year. Which means "next." No one wants to be a next.

It's about being organic and fresh every time.

I saw the Rolling Stones at TCF Stadium in Minneapolis. I was absolutely blown away because after 50 years of performing together they've had every experience there is. They've gone as high as you possibly can and they're in their 70s. Yet they didn't call it in. They performed every song like it's the first time they'd ever done it, and like it might be the last time the four of them get to do it. I just thought that was incredible for them to be so present, so excited to perform for 45,000 people and not have it be just one more show on the tour. You don't have to be the Rolling Stones to pull it off. As a speaker, you want the audience to feel like they're the only audience you have that year. You don't want to tell them, I just came in from a presentation yesterday and I have to leave early because I have to catch a flight to go to another presentation. I've heard speakers say that, and I think it's a turn off for the audience. To give yourself the freedom to be open and real, treat this as the first and last one you might ever have.

Is there anything specific you do right before you speak?

I walk the back room to look at the audience and see how the room sounds. I take a sheet of paper and write my outline every time so that it's in my coat pocket when I go up on the stage. Not that I'm going to pull it out and look at it, but to write down what my show set is. Like a band. I put myself in the mindset of trying to understand at this time of day, in this room, what type of energy they need in order to be open to the message. It's more about me trying to get a feel for the audience than it is about me psyching myself up.

What's the worst thing that's happened to you as a speaker? You must have had many experiences, having spoken so long.

Where do want to start, Maria? I can go through a quick list.

What comes to mind first?

Students blowing up a condom like a beach ball and having it bounce in the gymnasium as I'm speaking. Right before I'm introduced there's a bat that's flying around in a circle about six feet above the kids' heads. In this gymnasium. The principal saying just go ahead. I can't go on with a bat.

No kidding.

Being at a corporate event with a pizza chain in California and having an earthquake with the screen behind me shaking, and me not knowing that there's an earthquake going on, but then realizing that there's an earthquake going on. A fire alarm in the first third of your presentation where everybody has to leave the room and then they come back in and you start up again. All the lights going out because a power generator blew. Somebody falling over in the third row like they had a heart attack, which is tougher than the back row.

Wow. How does anyone prepare for that?

Every speaker should have a go-to list of what to do if this happens. What do I do if somebody raises their hand in the middle of my presentation, stands up and asks me a question. How do I handle that? What do I do when the sound goes out? What's my backup plan? What do I do if the lights go out? You must have a list and know what action to take.

So, what *do* you do when the sound goes out?

Depending on the room, I will continue without a microphone if the room allows. Then, I will switch out my stories to ones that aren't as reliant on amplification or a character's voice. When I was in schools, I'd talk to the sound crew beforehand and insist that I need a mic and a backup mic. "Oh, you won't need a backup mic, this thing works great." I would insist: "No, I really do need it. There's a 98% chance you're right, but there's a 2% chance that if something goes out I'll need a backup mic." I tell the sound crew, "Okay, if we get a gremlin today I'll go to the podium mic while you run up another handheld mic for me, or better yet, have another handheld mic under the podium that I can grab." "Okay."

What have you learned about setting up speaking gigs and working with the event planners?

I've always wanted to be known as easy to work with. If I come in to a room and it's set up, I'm not going to say at the last minute, "Oh, you need to move this around," or "People can't be at rounds, I need them to be in theater seating." We make some recommendations for what we're going to need on our website. For instance, if you have an audience of 100 people you're going to need to get some lighting on the stage in a hotel ballroom. I've been in a hotel ballroom and without the lighting it's absolutely dark. There are 500 people there and you can't see past the fifth row and half the audience can't even make out your face. That happens to you once. I hear from some event planners that some people are pretty demanding or they switch things around. And again, I came from 20 years of performing in schools where the situations were not always good. So, you do the best with what you have. Now, I'm in Marriott ballrooms and I've got a sound crew and a lighting crew and there's a stage and they have water for you.

It's all relative, right?

It's all relative. I can't believe people get into the profession and all of a sudden they're on the fast track and they have people picking them up at the airport, they're staying at nice hotels. Everything works. It's like, pay your dues. Or just be very appreciative of what you have.

How do you manage requests with the meeting planners?

You put it in your contract: in an audience of 100 people or more there must be some stage lighting. Then you talk to the staff, and ask what it costs to rent a couple of spotlights. Just lights on a tree in the back of the room. It's anywhere from $300 to $500. Then you tell the meeting planner it's going to cost you $500 to get some lighting in there. It's one of the best things you could do. Then you give the event planner ideas like, in order to put me in the best light and to make this an impactful event for your audience, you need to ensure these things happen. You learn from each experience.

What do you love about speaking?

I love being able to connect with an audience. I love to make them laugh, hit an emotion, give them a different perspective or remind them of something they forgot. I try to be different, and I'm terrified of looking and sounding the same as everybody else that's out there. I love to have a message that people are going to remember a day, a week, a month, a year, ten years later. I just received an email from a guy that heard me back in 1987 at a conference in Massachusetts when he was a sophomore in high school. He had attended my breakout session and there was something that happened in the presentation that day that encouraged him to take risks which helped him chart his own path in this world. The most rewarding thing is to have a message that is going to elicit an emotion, thought, or perspective within an audience member.

That is such a great story. What do you think today most speakers miss? What would be your top piece of advice?

My wife Susan, fellow speaker and friend Eric Chester, and I have started an intense speaker training experience called Keynote Kamp where we train speakers for a long weekend. What I've heard from Lou Heckler, an amazing speech coach, and what we've discovered after running these camps, is that most people are actually missing clarity of message, a premise. Where do I want to go, how do I get there and how does this relate to the audience? I know it sounds so elementary, but I've seen people wander off onto tangents and lose focus on why they're there.

That's great advice. Mark, if you knew then what you know now, what you have done differently?

I would approach my career with more confidence, with different audiences. On the other hand, I'm a firm believer that you have to earn it every step along the way by throwing yourself into a little bit bigger audience, a little tougher setting, an audience that doesn't react verbally as much as you'd hoped. But you get through it. For example, I was at a conference with the top 50 cardiac surgeons from across the U.S. It was the most intimidating presentation I would ever have. The audience, we're talking Harvard, Stanford, Mayo Clinic, brilliant surgeons, and all I keep hearing in my head is, St. Cloud State, St. Cloud State, St. Cloud State.

Oh no.

It scared the bejeebers out of me. That night I spoke to the surgeons and their partners and spouses. They could save lives and do open heart surgery, but I realized they struggled with family connections, priorities, dealing with their staff, and making better connections. The talk went better than I had hoped and I walked away with a lot more confidence. It's like a little kid going on the street riding a bike with their mom and dad, taking their hands off and feeling this joy of hey, I did it.

What's your advice for someone getting into speaking?

Find your hook. Nice bike is a hook. "A" it's my premise, "B" it's our brand, "C" it's how people remember me. No one says, "Oh, I heard Mark Scharenbroich speak." No one. Not even my relatives. People say, who'd you hear? I heard the nice bike guy. Nice bike, yeah. He talks about connecting with other people.

And you didn't get it right away, you went through several iterations. Right?

It took us a long time before we really settled in on it. How's an audience member going to remember you? When they walk away from a presentation and they say, "Yeah, I really enjoyed the speech." "What did they talk about?" "I don't know, but it was really good. Talked about relationships." No. You want somebody to come up to you with your hook. You need a hook they will remember.

I want to thank you again for your time, Mark. This has been wonderful.

You're welcome, Maria. It's been a pleasure.

KEY TAKEAWAYS

- Take the audience on an emotional roller coaster ride.
- Tell powerful stories to open up the audience and get them to listen to what's next.
- Know your material well so you can observe the audience.
- Have a clear premise that drives everything in your talk.
- Find your hook.

ABOUT MARK SCHARENBROICH

Mark's path started when he founded a comedy troupe that performed at high schools and colleges. His speaking career kicked into gear when he was featured in the award-winning Jostens film, "The Greatest Days of Your Life So Far," which has been shown to more than 10,000 high schools worldwide. Mark became known for being able to grab the attention of 2,500 students in a gymnasium in 30 seconds or less. His ability to connect with students and keep them glued to the presentation with humor and life-changing messages, earned him a reputation for being the top speaker in education. When the comedy troupe disbanded, he went solo, combining his comedy with leadership training. The demand for Mark as a speaker skyrocketed and he left his marketing position at Jostens in 1984. Mark has won the Axiom Business Book Award, the Ben Franklin Book Award, and is a National Speakers Association Hall of Fame inductee.

CONTACT:

You can learn more about Mark at his website www.nicebike.com, which has videos, a blog, and information on how to purchase his book, Nice Bike. He and his wife Susan also do a speaking camp once a year which you can learn about on the website. You can also follow Mark on social media.

CHAPTER 4:
SCOTT SCHWEFEL

"For someone to be truly successful they need to align their skills and passion in the marketplace in a way that serves the world."
-Scott Schwefel

 Scott Schwefel is an international speaker, author and trainer. He works with organizations who want to leverage new communication strategies to increase sales, profits, and productivity. Scott has spoken to over 1,000 companies, teaching them how to "Communicate in Full Color," for sales people, leaders, and teams. For over a decade, Scott has been speaking and teaching new communication strategies to companies and associations globally. His company was named one of the 50 fastest-growing private companies in Minnesota in 1997 and 1998, and he was named in Minnesota's 40 Under 40 list of successful top executives. Scott is a Certified Speaking Professional (CSP), a designation in the National Speakers Association that only 10% of all speakers receive.

Welcome. It's great to have you here, Scott.

Hi, Maria. Thanks for having me. I'm glad to be here.

Congratulations on your CSP designation.

Thank you very much.

Take us back to the beginning. How did you start out as a speaker?

About 23 years ago, I got thrust into the speaking world because I was running a technology company that had a significant level of growth. I was asked to speak about the success that our business was having. At that time, I was very uncomfortable getting in front of groups, teams, even a group of 10 or 15 people. In fact, after trying it a few times I realized I was so uncomfortable in that setting that I began to send my sales manager and sort of backed away from that potential opportunity. At the same time, I realized it was a gap in my skillset and I had to fix it.

What steps did you take to start building those skills?

Toastmasters turned out to be the beginning of my journey to become a confident speaker in front of groups. I spent many years attending the weekly meetings, practicing, and beginning to hone the craft. While running my technology business and working with so many different people, I realized I had a passion around personality styles. So, I began to teach courses on that topic. Very small, 10, 15, 20 students, in evening programs while I was running my technology business during the day. That was the beginning of presenting on the topics I still speak to today.

I'm sure many people can relate to the difficulty you had when you began speaking. After you started going to Toastmasters, what did you do differently?

That's a great question because it has different answers based on who you talk with. I spent a significant amount of time and money working with coaches and companies so I could become a better public speaker. I knew doing that would create some great opportunities for me in the future. Getting out there and speaking helped me overcome that fear. But some of the coaches I worked with said, "To be a great speaker, you have to be able to speak on any topic. You need to project and convey passion around the topic no matter how you feel about it." And that was one school of coaching I got. Another group came back and said, "You know what, if you're not passionate about the topic, you should not be speaking about it. If you want to be a great speaker, you should only speak about things that you've got great deal of passion for." These were literally two different coaching approaches all within a one-year timeframe. I stepped back and wondered, what in the world is the right answer?

So, what happened?

Fortunately, I found a topic that I am truly passionate about. Helping people show up in a better way, and understand what they're good at, is my sweet spot. I do this by understanding unique personality styles, how people are wired, what makes them tick, and how they communicate with others. That topic has also inspired the books I've written. And quite honestly, if I'm called on to speak about another topic I'm not personally vested in, I'm not able to present the material to the level I do now. As long as I'm speaking in alignment with that topic, I am able to bring my full self and my full passion into all the work that I do.

I can hear your passion around this as you talk. What difference does it make to speak from your passion and authentic self versus performing or trying to be something you're not?

I put speakers in two different categories. One is folks like me that speak about what we do because we have passion around it, regardless of the group we may be in front of. But there's another category of speaker that can take a message that resonates well with people, and regardless of their interest in the topic, demonstrate it in a powerful way. I spend a lot time interacting with other speakers, and the majority of them speak on a topic about which they have a tremendous amount of passion.

So, the key is to find something you're passionate about.

Yes. But, here's what most people miss: it must be something you're passionate about that also fills some sort of need in the marketplace. As you know, running around passionate about something that nobody else cares about, in terms of financial viability, is just not going to work. It's got to be a topic that you love, and you can't just talk about it. You need to demonstrate it and be good at it. The passion I've had around understanding self and others, which is the core of all communication, has taken me into a focus around leadership. The number of CEOs I've personally worked with now tops 2,000. And these are folks that have been through a lot of training, and a lot of coaching. Yet, this message of understanding self and others resonates with leaders and their sales people and teams.

How is doing a keynote different from walking into a Fortune 500 company and delivering a training session with CEOs?

There are some similarities and differences. The commonality is the topic. And, the target audience may sometimes be the same, but what's happened in the last couple years is the line between the two has blurred. I'll do a 60-minute keynote for 1,000 people, and I might walk them through the key concepts of our program, which is around personality styles, using a four-quadrant color-coded model. We use the Insights Discovery Profile. I've also taken groups as large as 500 through a three-hour, in-depth learning program. And I've delivered a one-hour keynote to groups of 10, 15, 20, or 25 people. So, it's hard to say, where do you draw the line between what's a keynote today and what's a facilitated, in-depth learning and training session?

Describe some of the speaking situations that you approach differently.

In a learning program, I help the audience build awareness around the concept. Especially in big sales or leadership conferences, the audience learns the model, and then identifies themselves using tools like wristbands, and putting colors on their name tags. That drives how they interact with each other, and they have enough of an awareness to use it. That's an exciting keynote-type presentation. There's also taking a leadership team for three or six hours, into an in-depth understanding of these same concepts, which is a much deeper learning experience. Those are the two sides of what I do.

You manage to pull in the audience and engage them with humor, stories, and your natural personality. What techniques do you use to connect in that authentic way?

That's a great question. I don't know if it's a technique as much as an unlearning of what I learned incorrectly in the first place. My partner and wife, Linda, who's always been an exceptional public speaker, we used to tease each other, more in particular her teasing me, because as I was beginning down this path of trying to become a better speaker, I tried to act like what I thought a better speaker would look like. And we've had a running joke for 25 years with a celebrity on The Today Show from many years back that used to come on and present herself in a very unnatural way. She'd start out every newscast by saying enthusiastically, "Good morning, everybody!" And as soon as she did it, you'd go, that's not real. That's not her. Why doesn't she just say, "Good morning, everyone," in whatever her most natural mode would be? And at that moment, I realized that I was trying to be a speaker that same way. I was trying to act like I thought a speaker should act.

What did that change look like for you?

Fortunately, when I began to find a topic about which I felt a real sense of passion, understanding and a good skillset, I was able to let all that pretending fall away. I can't tell you for sure when it disappeared. There was a point where I stopped feeling the need to pretend like I was a speaker, and I just naturally spoke to people. And now, whether I'm with five people or 5,000 people, I'm able to just communicate with them, almost in the same way I would communicate with you right now in this conversation. I've got an understanding of a great topic I'm passionate about it, and I'm really eager to make sure that you can walk away and understand it and use it. And those feelings can be applied to five or 5,000.

So many people want to get to that place. What does it take to get there?

It's really about stripping away this notion of pretending to be a speaker or pretending to show up a certain way, and instead allowing your true self to come through. Which, as easy as it sounds to just be yourself when you speak, I think it's one of the hardest things to do. Because it's the stripping away and the dropping off of everything else that gets in the way.

And making yourself vulnerable to the audience.

Yeah, you have to be real. I think that's a great point. I think people are worried about being vulnerable, so they try and build a wall in front of themselves, or they put on a mask of, "I'm a speaker, and I'm going to power through this, but for God's sake, don't ask me a question in the middle of it or I'll totally lose my place and crack." It's really just, "Hey, I'm up here, and let's have a conversation." And I've found a comfort level in having a conversation with 1,000 people, because that's what it is. It's just a conversation.

That's a great attitude. You're a successful speaker, trainer and author. How did you build up each area, and what advice do you have for others to build up these different profit centers?

There was this sales manager from 30 years ago that I had, and on the wall he had a plaque that said, "nothing happens anywhere, anytime, for any reason, until somebody, somewhere, somehow, sells something." And I've never forgotten that poster. Because that's where it starts. You can be brilliant. But, unless you can find a way to get the message to people that it helps them solve a problem of some kind, they may not want to hear from you. Ultimately, you've got to have a mindset that says, "I want to be a great speaker, so I'm going to have to sell something." Which doesn't mean a used car sales guy in plaid pants trying to steal your wallet. "I'm somebody that's got a great message that can help you solve problems I believe you might have. I just need a chance to talk with you about it."

Sometimes people cringe when they hear "selling." But the truth is, we're always selling, even if it's selling others to believe in what we have to say. It's about opening up a space for the other person to be able to accept something you have that might help improve their life.

Oh, absolutely. I'm a huge fan of Daniel Pink, and I just finished his newest book, "To Sell Is Human." He talks about the way people used to view sales and sales people, the old game of sales guy has knowledge, you need it, so he can sneak up on you and trick you and get you to sign on the dotted line. Those days are gone. Because of the universal access to information, selling today is about, "how can I help create a mutual benefit for you that I'm involved in?" It's a completely different conversation. And people that have always said, I hate selling, or I hate sales people, are now able to say, "I love talking to people, because I genuinely want to understand what problems they are trying to solve, and what, if anything, I can do to help them solve those problems." That's a whole new paradigm of selling.

Yeah, it is a shift. Often, when someone is selling some sort of program or service, they awkwardly switch into selling mode at the end. It can be a much more natural flow into, what conversation can we have about this?

You're right, it's a paradigm shift. And the easiest thing to think about is, if somebody just replaces the word *sell* with the word *share*. Right? What do I do? I've got to sell my program. Actually, no, you've got to share your program. You've got to share with other people what your program is, genuinely care about what problems they might have, and genuinely figure out if what you're sharing will help solve their problem. Because if it does, you'll want to do something with me, and if it doesn't, you won't. So, that subtle shift from sell to share, for a lot of people, changes everything.

That's a great idea. Just shifting words can change your entire mindset. You had a pretty cool experience living with the Hadza and Maasai tribes in Africa. What was that like, and how did it impact you personally and professionally?

The gentleman who takes that trip every year is Richard Leider, one of my all-time favorite authors, and now a good friend as a result of that experience. Richard has written many books that are all about doing your life's work. After reading his books and hearing him speak several times, the message was, are you doing what you would do if you had all the money in the world or no money? At the time, I was having great success in my technology business, but I stepped back and realized, this is going well, but I'm not really passionate about it. I'm not sure if it's truly leveraging my skillset, even though the market really seems to want it. So, after eight or nine years of success in that business, I chose to go on that trip with Richard, to intentionally get out there and live with those tribes with the goal of forgetting a number of things.

What was it like when you first got there?

This is what many of us do, when we travel we all take our one week vacation, and we end up still thinking about work the whole time, unfortunately. And that's what we did the first week in Africa. And then the second week, work actually starts to drift out of the picture, and you start thinking about your family. We were 2,000 miles out in the middle of nowhere. No phones, no communication, no clocks. And your mind starts to shift. About 14, 16 days in, you start to forget your whole life. And about 23,

24 days into the event, you start to forget who you are. You're just sitting around a fire of most of the day, and you arrive at a comfort level where you don't talk much. Near the end of that trip, you'd wake up and basically just exist without thinking about who you are. It's as close as I could get to not thinking consciously about anything. It was the one time in my life where my brain emptied itself of rambling thoughts.

That sounds amazing.

And then Richard, in a very skilled way, would start to talk with you. Toward the end of the trip he'd say, hey, if you could be anything, what would you want to be? And you really were coming at it from a blank slate. And that was the moment when I realized, hey, if I could do anything, if I didn't have any other restrictions in my life, this is something I love. I'm passionate about it. I've got a skillset for it. And by the way, the marketplace is going to need it forever. I had worked with and taught courses using Myers-Briggs™ and DISC and other assessments, but when I found Insights Discovery™, there was something about that group in Scotland and that assessment that enabled me to piece it all together. And so, part of my conversation with Richard was about, is there something that I could bring to the marketplace that everybody wants and needs, that I love, that I'm good at delivering, and anybody, in any business, at any level, could purchase from me? That was what drove me into doing what I do today.

What was it like when you got back to real life?

When I came back from that trip, it was a real immersion back into what seemed like a crazy and frantic world. But, at the same time I was fully committed to selling my technology business and moving into the work I do today.

That sounds like a wonderful experience, to empty your head because so much information bombards us. And it sounds like

you were living in the moment, with no ego, which so often gets in our way.

Well, yeah, it does. But, you don't have to go to Africa to experience this. You don't have to live with a hunter-gatherer tribe for a month to get there. For some people, they're able to sit down and meditate 15 minutes every morning and get back to that place of square one. That's what it's all about, if we all were at square one again and we could wake up and look out and say, I think I'll do whatever I want today, what would it be? And people create this limitation mindset, and that's what a lot of my books speak about. I'd do this if I could, but I can't because of these limitations.

So, if you're about to go speak, you can take that same approach. You empty your mind and say, what could I do here? What could I offer? How could I take advantage of this amazing experience, and what could I offer with this blank slate?

Yeah, and you're going to have to be real. That's the catch. You can't fake that. I know it's a joke from Woody Allen, right, "When you learn how to fake authenticity, you've got it made." I really don't think you can. You've got to be up there with real content, real purpose and real intent, because the world picks up on that.

What advice would you have for someone trying to build up a speaking business? Because you're not just a speaker. You own a business.

I think it's dangerous to think of yourself as just a speaker, right? Versus a business owner. Part of that business is you speaking, but there needs to be more to your business. I know many speakers who think, when I launch that book it's all going to come together. But that's a rare speaker that surpasses that speaking income with what they've published. You can also look at doing training, speaking, or coaching. What's the business model that can be wrapped around what you're speaking about?

I've been able to build a training company underneath me that is able to contract other very talented trainers to go in and give you that in-depth work. So, while I'm a full-time professional speaker, I'm also a full-time businessman running a training business that is coupled with the keynotes that I do. Your ability to get out there and talk to large groups and then have follow-up training or coaching opportunities is a good business model. It's not impossible to make a great living just as a keynote speaker. But, just know that as long as you're doing it, you're traveling, and you're speaking. I'm upwards of 100,000 miles every year. I won't do that forever, but that's what it takes if you're committed and really want to move forward in the speaking arena.

What would you say to somebody who's starting out speaking, but having trouble finding speaking gigs?

If you've got something you want to talk about, get out and talk about it. There are so many opportunities to speak, and monthly meetings for so many groups. Toastmasters is a brilliant place to learn. But from every Lions Club, Rotary, Kiwanis, church and non-profit, there are thousands of opportunities to test your message in front of groups. It's got to convey a benefit for them, and you've got to practice to make sure you're ready for the first group that brings you in for very low wages. That's how you start, right? And you work your way up. Supply and demand is no different in the speaking arena than anywhere else. You've got to get those folks and groups and corporations to want your message and to want you.

One of the things speakers get really good at is being flexible and just going with the flow, because anything can happen. I imagine by now you've had just about everything happen. What was the worst thing that happened to you and how did you recover?

Great question. I can't count the number of times I would show up somewhere, and all the materials I needed to run the session simply didn't make it. In one case I showed up to take a couple dozen CEOs through a three-hour intensive training program, and my office confirmed the materials had been delivered. But the day before I arrived, somebody there looked at it, saw my name and said, this guy doesn't work here, and then shipped them back.

Oh no! What did you do?

In that moment, it's about improvising. And it was working with my team to send electronic versions of all the profiles we needed. I literally had only one sample of the tools that I would have had for everyone, so I had to demonstrate without their ability to use them and work with them in practice. Sometimes you have to improvise. The first time I ever delivered a program using PowerPoint, I realized the projector had died, and we were on a retreat out in the middle of nowhere. Could I improvise? Could I pull it off? And what you realize is that when you let people know what you're trying to do, they'll support you and work with you. What you don't want to do is fake it. You don't want to pretend you know how it's going to turn out. You don't want to put up that mask or that wall and pretend that you're some genius behind a curtain. Because you're not. You're somebody that got stuck, short, trapped, showed up at the wrong place or showed up hours later, missed a flight or couldn't get a flight in on time. And you just do what you have to do. It's all about improvising in an authentic way. Let somebody know what you're working with, what you're dealing with, and pull it off. And when people know that you're genuine and that you're trying, they'll give you the support that you need.

The audience wants you to succeed. It's about shaking it off and getting back into that centered place of, how can I serve them? And not letting yourself ruminate over the mistake.

I think people don't realize just how much they're capable of until they're pushed. I had a client over in Europe, and they wanted me to come over and deliver our program. And at the time, this was 10, 11 years ago, the goal was a full-day workshop to teams throughout Europe. So, it was five days in a row, delivering an all-day program in five different cities that were located in three different countries. The juggling and the transportation was insane. On one of those legs of that journey, all of a sudden the train broke down. The next morning we arrived at 7 am, and I was on at 8 o'clock. I hadn't slept at all, so I jumped right in the shower, cleaned up, got ready, and dove out there, and did another full day. And then, hopped a plane, and went to another one. And at the end of the week, I looked back at what I had done and I thought, oh my gosh, that's amazing to pull that off.

Kind of changes your perspective.

I used to complain if I had two workshops back-to-back. Or, my gosh, what about three days back-to-back in two or three different locations? But when I was able to stretch to that extent, ever since then, every week I look at my schedule and I say to myself, it's not that week. It's not five cities, three countries, and a broken train. Whatever it is, it's completely manageable and within my scope.

If you knew then what you know now, what would you have done differently?

I wouldn't have waited so long to get into the work that I love. Why did I avoid the risk? I love what I do so much that I'm a little bit panicked that I only have 20 or 30 years left, seriously. So, when I think about, what would I do differently, I would dive in faster, I'd start sooner. I'd still go in the exact same direction, but you can't ever go back. So, my advice is, if you're thinking about, you know, I kind of want to do this. I think I might want to do this. The answer is DO this. Find a way to make it happen.

Scott, thanks so much for your time. This has been a really great conversation.

Absolutely, Maria. Great talking with you, and thanks for having me.

KEY TAKEAWAYS

- Find something you're passionate about that fills a need in the marketplace.
- Stop pretending to be a speaker and instead let your true self come through.
- Replace the word "sell" with "share."
- Find your way back to square one.
- Don't fake it. Improvise in an authentic way.

ABOUT SCOTT SCHWEFEL

A serial entrepreneur, Scott founded and grew Minnesota's largest technology training company to over 12 million in sales, and then sold the company in 2003. Scott also founded and grew Insight's Twin Cities to over $3 million in sales and sold it to Insights in Scotland in 2014. He is a published author, has lived remotely with the Hadza and Maasai tribes in Tanzania, Africa and is a top-rated speaker for Vistage, the largest membership organization of CEOs in the world. Scott has personally trained and coached over 2,000 CEOs. He has presented in Paris, London, Amsterdam, Geneva, Shanghai, and even Kuwait.

CONTACT

To learn more about Scott's keynote speaking, visit his website at www.scottschwefel.com, where you'll find one of Scott's books available to download as a free gift. For information about Scott's corporate sales training, team building, and leadership development, visit www.discoveryourself.com. Scott is active on social media.

CHAPTER 5:
LISA SASEVICH

"Make sure what you're doing is meaningful and attach it to that which is meaningful to you. "
-Lisa Sasevich

Lisa Sasevich is known as the Queen of Sales Conversion and teaches experts who are making a difference how to get their message out and enjoy massive results without being salesy. She's been honored with the Distinguished Mentor Award from the Business Expert Forum at the Harvard Faculty Club and is a recipient of the coveted eWomen Network Foundation Champion Award for her generous fundraising. Lisa's also been ranked on the prestigious Inc. 500/5000 list of America's Fastest Growing Private Companies for two years in a row.

Welcome, Lisa. Thank you so much for being here today.

My pleasure. Thanks for having me.

Tell us a little bit about your story. If you go back to the beginning, how did it all start?

It all started when I was working at a company that I just loved. It was a personal development company. I thought I would be there forever, and I was kind of the right hand to the owner. But, to my surprise, I was fired and it was shocking timing. It was like the night before Christmas Eve. I had a three-year-old and I would soon have a newborn on the way, so it was that time of life when you're juggling the maximum number of things at their most sensitive time. It really caused me to go into sort of a dark night of the soul. I felt like I was contributing my gift and talents at that company. I couldn't think of how else or where else I could do that.

So, what did you do?

Somehow, in the middle of all that and the exploration of what I was going to do next, maybe it was inspired by my trusted source, I decided to just get out there and give. I didn't know exactly what my gift was, but I knew I had helped build a lot of companies. I knew how to make more sales, get more clients, and do it in a way that felt good, so I just started talking about that. It was really from getting out there and sharing that I realized what a miraculous and low-tech way it was to be able to share my gift and make my offer, my invitation, to more than one person at a time.

What did your business look like in those early days?

I would speak to small groups and contribute some content, some value. I didn't have my brand all figured out. I mean, I didn't have any products. I had an AOL email account and I could take a check in my name. I didn't have any of the things that you see today, but I would speak and then, before I finished up, I would make an invitation. Sometimes, the invitation would be like $297 for an hour of coaching with me so we could figure out your offer, right? People who'd never heard my name, didn't know me from Adam, got enough value from my 45 minutes of speaking to say, "I would like to go ahead and make that investment and have a little more private attention from her on my work." That's really what led into it.

How did this evolve and grow into what you speak about today?

I never started speaking to be a speaker. I just got out there and started talking to groups. I thought of it more as sharing and contributing my knowledge and expertise, because I wanted to help my work get out there in a bigger way. A lot of people hear the word "speaking," and they discount themselves. Like, "That's not me. I'm not a speaker," at least in our client base. And when I say "speaker," I'm not necessarily talking about keynote speaking where you're really polished at presentation skills and you're actually selling the talk. My specialty now is in showing people how to get out there and speak for free, be yourself, be authentic, give from your heart and then have that talk structured in a way that leads to making your invitation or what we call your "irresistible offer."

Many heart-centered entrepreneurs and business owners begin by speaking for free and then offering something at the end. Were you nervous when you started offering things while speaking?

There's always that little voice in your head saying, "Is what I'm saying going to be valuable?" But, what I learned, and I feel like this is just so helpful and you already hit one of the keys is, when I was in that giving place, it made me less nervous because my attention wasn't on me. I was focused on, "What can I provide today, what can I give?" That right there is probably one of the biggest known secrets to getting over being nervous; shifting your attention to what you can give to your audience instead of worrying about, "Am I good enough or is my content good enough?"

Yes, and it's so easy to get hooked into that thinking when you're starting out.

I know, right? The other thing that I came to see, and it's amazing, but the thing that would be easiest and most natural for you to speak about, is your gift, because it's so easy and natural for you. But, just because it's easy and natural for you doesn't mean that it's easy and natural for other people. In fact, in many cases, it's the thing that does come most easily to you that makes other people wonder, "How do you do that?" I would share how to make your offer irresistible, which I just love to do. To me, it was just so obvious and easy, but other people would say, "Oh, my gosh, I need to work with you more. This will change my whole business." What I would share is that, for anyone who's in an expertise-based business, you're a service professional, you're working in your gift or your blessing or your talent, be on the lookout because the thing that you'll get booked the most for and that you'll get paid the most for is probably the thing that is the easiest for you to do. It's a little counterintuitive, right?

Yes, and sometimes it's so close us, we don't know that it's an expertise. What would you say to people who are saying, "I don't know what to talk about. What's my gift?"

If you're not sure what your gift is, take a look at the people that you help. I call it your million-dollar value. Look around your life and think about people that you've helped or that thing that people come to you for all the time. It seemed to me that anytime one of my friends would get into a new multilevel or network marketing, they always would come to me. They wanted me in their down line. I mean, I had this sense that there was something I was good at around networking and getting the word out and inspiring people to act. Look to see what people come to you for, or look at people you've helped and then try to hone in on one, like, "I helped Janet, and if I could help a hundred or a thousand people just like Janet, that would be a life well-spent." Right? That's how you can start honing in on your million-dollar value.

When did you feel a turning point? What was your first big speaking gig like?

My biggest gig was about 13,000 people in a stadium, but that wasn't my turning-point big gig. My big turning-point gig was 60 people in Santa Barbara at a speakers' boot camp. I was living in Tucson where I had a newborn and a three-year-old, and I left them with a nanny, got on a plane and flew away from my kids to Santa Barbara. I was doing the talk I had been doing locally in Tucson, which I call my "Speak to Sell" talks. It was my first night away from my kids, and the first time I spoke on a stage outside of my hometown. So, the turning point was flying somewhere and doing that talk on another stage. The exact same talk, but done in a new city with a new audience that didn't know me. I did my talk and made my offer and, not in a year, not in a month, not in a week, but in 90 minutes, I made $10,000.

Wow.

12 people said, "Oh, my gosh, I'd love to work with you more," and they signed up. They said "yes" to my invitation on the spot. I remember going back to my room that night, it was a cabin up in the mountain, we were at a retreat center, and thinking, "This was amazing. I love these new clients. I love speaking with them. I love sharing, and I can't wait to give them more. How can I do this all the time?" I mean, this is going to change my family, my legacy, my kids' lives. It was actually at that moment that I connected with something that my dad had said to me before he passed away. This came from his life as a world-famous ventriloquist. He had an act and he had his dummy, and he went all around the world with this one act and he became famous making people laugh and feel good. I mean, famous, like he was on The Ed Sullivan Show twice.

That's really cool.

His name was Eddie Garson. He said this thing to me before he passed away, and this was my turning point. He said, "Lisa, don't change your act. Change your audience." And it was really at that point that I said, "Oh, my God, I did my act in Tucson in all these local places. Now, I just did my act in Santa Barbara and I made $10,000 and got 12 new clients." I realized my whole entrepreneurial business was just taking my Speak to Sell talk and getting it in front of as many ideal clients that are already gathering. So, instead of doing what most entrepreneurs do, where you create a new act for every talk, I have my one Speak to Sell talk. Sure, I tweak it to fit different audiences here and there, but for nearly ten years I've been doing that talk in front of different audiences and inspiring people now in 134 countries to come and say "yes," do our work, and get their Speak to Sell talk and their irresistible offers dialed in.

A key thing you said is making the offer, and so many people get stuck there. They talk and then they don't open up and say, "Here's what I have. Here's my gift."

Yeah, it's so true.

Many people have this outdated perspective on selling, but we're always selling. Why is it so important to shift our thinking around making our offer?

Yeah, it's such an important question, Maria. I really appreciate it. I think there are two reasons. One has to do with the world. The world needs you, right? If you don't make your offer, how can people who are loving what you're saying, eating it up like water in the desert, how can they get more? How can they take it further if you don't make your offer? Those are the obvious reasons, but there's another reason to make your offer. A lot of people don't think about this. If you don't make your offer, it's kind of like you are out there doing the heavy lifting for your competition. You are the advertisement. You're telling people they need an estate plan, or they need to redecorate their home, or they need a coach, or they need something in the areas of health or relationships. You're the one spreading the word. You're opening possibility, but if you don't make an offer, there's no door for anybody to step through. It causes you to be inspirational, which is great, but not transformational, which is really where that long and lasting value comes in.

That's a great perspective. You've become very successful as a speaker. What did it take to get to that level and what would you say to someone who's trying to get there?

It's funny, but even to this day, while I am featured on Speaker Magazine and I speak at the National Speakers Association, and I know that I am largely seen in the world of speaking, the funny part is I have not studied presentation skills. My love and my answer to how to get there is structure. I believe structure gives you freedom. My work is respected among the speaking community because professional speakers understand they're selling their speaking. It's the structure. It's what makes them magnificent and on demand over and over. The structure I'm talking about is not about showing up polished. It's about structuring how you get the results that you get in the world. Whether it's in the areas of health, business, relationship, or money, there's a system behind what you do and a way that you make that special thing that is yours to provide.

What's the worst thing that's happened to you as a speaker and how did you recover?

Oh, it's a really good question. Let me see. This is kind of a funny angle to it, but one of the worst things that happens to me as a speaker is when I can't make an offer. When I'm up there teaching people how to make an offer, how to inspire an on-the-spot yes, and I'm not allowed to make an offer, I feel like I'm talking about something that I can't model. I have a great story you'll appreciate here. Brian Tracy is one of my students and now, my friend, and he recommended me to the National Speakers Association. So, I got the privilege of speaking there two conferences in a row. I kept trying to put together this talk on irresistible offers without making one because they have a no-offer policy. You could speak, but you couldn't make an offer. I worked for weeks trying to put together a talk about making offers that were juicy, but I couldn't make one. It took away the magic. I got up on the stage, and it was a fully-packed room. Brian was sitting right in the front to empower me. I came up with a solution, and I saw him turn every shade of white as I did this. I said, "Look, I want to teach you guys how to make offers. But you know, talking about it without doing it, it just loses something in the translation. So, I want you all to stand up. Everybody raise your right hand, and I want you to repeat after me." And I had them say, "No matter how compelling Lisa Sasevich is with her offer, I promise not to buy from her today." They all took an oath, and then I was able to do my whole talk, make my offer, and hand out the order form. It said something like, "Sample purposes only," and I gave them the talk and the offer and it was awesome.

That's hilarious. Yeah, how do you talk about doing it and show them without actually doing it?

Right, it just lost all the steam. That was fun.

You are so comfortable and natural when you speak on stage. What do you recommend for others to become more comfortable?

Practice helps, but for me, it's back to structure. We usually see speakers in one of two ends of the spectrum. Either they're worried and nervous, so they script everything. I call them the scripters, and when you do that you're not present. You're worried that you're going to forget. If you miss a line, you lose where you are and it's stiff, so it just doesn't feel good to you or your audience. Other times, people will swing to the other end of the spectrum, and I call them wingers. They're winging it. They're going to stare into the eyes of the crowd and get the divine download on what to say. While there's nothing wrong with that gift, what can give you the space to feel confident and authentic is to use structure. Don't be a scripter. Don't be a winger. Be a structurer. You can use slides to keep you on track, so you know the next points or story you're going to tell, but you feel free to converse with the guy in the second row or crack a joke because something funny just happened. Or, you can say a thought that's passing through your mind because you know you can find your way back to the structure.

What's the first thing you do right when you walk out on stage?

I look around. I feel the energy. If I'm in a room that needs to be lifted a bit, I'll bring the energy up. I try to match the frequency of the room and connect in that way. The thing I do before I step on to the stage is to get very connected to what I call the PSPS. It stands for problem, solution, problem, solution. I get connected to, "what is the problem that my talk is going to solve?" In many cases, I'm talking about how to make your offer irresistible and that's the first PS, problem solution. So, my talk is going to help you make your offer irresistible, and then I get really clear on the second PS, which is, "what's the problem they're still going to have at the end of my talk?"

Can you give an example of that?

In many cases, it's, "Wow, you taught me how to make my offer irresistible. Now, I need to reverse engineer a talk that leads to that irresistible offer." So, the second S is the solution, and that's my invitation to join me, for example, in our Speak to Sell bootcamp. Knowing what problem I'm going to solve and what problem still exists that my work or offer helps solve allows me to focus on how I can best contribute to the audience at that moment. I am also helping people see what's ahead and what's possible as I'm making my invitation.

As you've become more successful over the years, how has your life changed and what has most surprised you?

The biggest thing that's changed, and that helped to cause the change, is feeling fulfilled because we tithe. We give. I give. I'm so grateful to God every day, I feel so blessed to be working in my blessing. I mean, I love the abundance, the money, the people, the acknowledgement. I love all of that, but what's more important is to be working every day in my blessing, and that's what I want for every single person is to wake up every day and just feel like, "Ahhh," just like eating my favorite dessert all day.

What led you to start focusing on that?

Some years ago, I stumbled onto the idea of giving 10% of everything that comes my way to people, places or institutions that feed me spiritually and remind me of who I am. I give, I tithe, I donate, but not based on need. I give based on inspiration. I give to that which I want to grow. It started out as an experiment. It was from a book I read called, *The Four Spiritual Laws of Prosperity* by Edwene Gaines. She suggested this experiment that you give 10% for six months. Now, this was the time in my life where my then husband was in fellowship to become a surgeon. We could barely pay our bills. We were sharing a car. Many times, it was hard to make rent. But, that's the time to do it, when it's a real stretch, where you're really showing God or your trusted source, you fill in the blank, that you are acknowledging something higher as a source of your good. We did the 6-month experience and I have to tell you. It brought such fulfillment to all the success. Making money is wonderful, but you have to make it fulfilling. My work is fulfilling, but being able to attach it to giving in this way is incredibly rewarding.

It sounds like this has been transforming for you.

It has. I've genuinely become a philanthropist over the last, say, eight years. I feel so blessed for that, too. My recommendation is to make sure what you're doing is meaningful and attach it to that which is meaningful to you. For many speakers, or people aspiring to use speaking to grow your business, you have a gift. You're creating the gift of having a public persona, of having a voice, and in many cases, a following. You can use that for so many good things in your work, making a difference in the world with projects and philanthropies and not-for-profits. I'm in my earning years, and I love that there are people out there doing things that I can contribute to that makes it all even more fulfilling.

I love that. When you make it bigger than yourself and you put energy out into the universe, it comes back around and becomes so much more fulfilling.

You said it, Maria.

Lisa, thank you so much for your time and for sharing your inspiring story.

Thank you, Maria, and thank you for the great work that you're doing.

KEY TAKEAWAYS

- When you shift into a place of giving, you become less nervous.
- You'll get booked and paid more for what comes most naturally to you, your gift.
- Don't change your act; change your audience.
- What can give you the space to feel confident and authentic is to use structure.
- You can use your speaking to really make a difference in the world.

ABOUT LISA SASEVICH

After 25 years of winning top sales awards and training senior executives at companies like Pfizer and Hewlett-Packard, Lisa left corporate America and put her skills to the test as an entrepreneur. She became very successful delivering high-impact, sales-closing strategies for turbo-charging entrepreneurs and small business owners, leading them to greater profits. In just a few short years, Lisa created a multimillion-dollar home-based business with two toddlers in tow, and that's no small feat. Lisa is the expert on how to make big money doing what you love.

CONTACT

You can find out more on Lisa's website, www.TheInvisibleClose.com. She's also offering a free gift called "The Irresistible Offer Blueprint." Go to: www.blueprintgift.com/maria to get the worksheet, the training, and Lisa's eZine. Lisa is on social media, including Facebook at www.LisaSasevichFan.com.

CHAPTER 6:
CRAIG VALENTINE

"It's the spaces between the lines that really make the story work."
-Craig Valentine

 Craig Valentine is an award-winning speaker and trainer, has traveled the world helping speakers, executives, and salespeople turn presentations into profits. Craig is President of The Communication Factory, LLC, which is an award-winning company that helps organizations profit by presenting with impact and persuading with ease. As a motivational speaker, he has spoken in over 20 countries giving as many as 160 presentations per year. Craig is the co-author of the Amazon #1 bestselling book, *World Class Speaking in Action*. He has received hundreds of speaking awards from Toronto to Taipei.

Welcome and thank you for being here, Craig.

Thank you for having me. I'm glad to be here with you.

Take us back to how it all started.

In 1994, I walked into a bookstore because my life was just going in the wrong direction, and I picked up a book called, *Live Your Dreams*, by Les Brown. After that, I read everything I could get my hands on in terms of public speaking.

What type of work did you do that led you to public speaking?

I became an event planner for a technology expo company. One of my jobs was to set up the stage for the speaker, taping down power, moving chairs, moving around the lectern. Every single time, I would stand behind the lectern and envision that one day the audience would show up for me. I would say to myself, "Today I move the chairs, tomorrow I move the audience." Thankfully tomorrow became today.

It sure did.

In 1998, I joined Toastmasters International and by 1999, I was the #1 World Champion of Public Speaking. That's really where it all started.

That's awesome. You have an MBA. How does this experience contribute to your speaking?

Initially, I saw myself as an artist rather than a business person. In fact, when I started in this business, I didn't want to market at all. I fought it. I said, I'm an artist. If people like my art, they'll hire me again. I fought it for at least five years. That's a year longer than the Civil War. That's a long fight. Then I woke up one morning and realized I was a starving artist. I left my PhD program and I said, I'm going to master marketing. I remember that year I read 62 books on marketing. Now, I love marketing.

Operating as a business can really help make speakers become more successful.

Like my friend Ed Tate says, "This is the speaking business." If you don't master the business, you don't get to speak.

How did you shift when you started to focus on marketing?

I read the book, *Permission Marketing* by Seth Godin. I learned people could contact me, I could offer them something free, and they could give me permission to market to them. That changed everything. I wasn't just blasting emails to people that don't want it, but to people that actually wanted to hear from me.

What else did you learn?

I realized it's about content. So, I made the decision, Maria. I said I'm going to be the biggest giver of free, valuable content for public speakers. When I made that decision, people just gravitated towards me. It's what some might call gravitational marketing. I haven't had to do a cold call in probably 16 years. I also integrated my sales background into everything I did. That made a big difference.

How did you use your sales background?

I don't sell the product. I sell the result. Whether it's back of the room sales, people reading my blog, listening to my speech, buying some of my courses, or reading my book. It's always about selling the result. For example, I remember when I went to buy a car early in my life and one of the salespeople tried to sell me a car. He said they have these types of windows and this type of engine and this and that. But, the other salesperson told me, "You're going to look gooood in that car. You're going to get the girls."

Yeah.

That's where I was like, "Where do I sign?" He made the sale not because he sold me the car, but because he sold me the results. When I was working with the publishing company, Glencoe/McGraw-Hill, the reason I was a three-time salesperson of the year was because the other salespeople were selling textbooks. I was selling test scores. Instead of saying, "Hey, look at this book, look how readable it is. Don't you like the colors? Don't you like this and that?" I was saying, "Do you want better test scores? If so, then follow this system." It's always about selling the results.

What do you feel was the big turning point for you in your speaking career?

I gave this speech in Montreal and it was awful. I remember going back to my hotel room that night, putting my head in the pillows and being ready to give up. That's when I called this lady who was supposed to be one of the best public speaking coaches in the country. I said, "Listen, I need a coach and I need to be coached by you." She said, "Are you sure?" I said, "Yes." When I heard the cost, I said, "Uh, I'm pretty happy with the skills that I have." But, then I realized that so many people look at the price of *doing* something, but they don't look at the cost of *not* doing it. So, she became my coach. I came to realize I was nowhere near where I needed to be as a speaker. That was my turning point. I went on a quest for reinventing myself as a speaker. That was 12 years ago, and it's been fantastic ever since.

When you started working with her, what did you notice about your speaking that makes you say, "I was nowhere near ready to be a speaker?"

It wasn't structured enough. She had a framework for her talks. I had pretty good stories, and I had learned to uncover some humor, but it wasn't structured to where you could walk out and remember my key points. When you get a coach, go to somebody who is strong where you're weak. Today, I'm probably one of the most structured speakers out there and if you ask people after my presentation, "What did he talk about?" They'll be able to say, boom, boom, boom. That was a result of working with her.

In your book, I noticed you cover "anchoring." What advice could you give around this concept?

What's loose is lost, which means when you're speaking, what's not tied to a story or some kind of anchor is going to be lost. An anchor is something that helps people remember the point. When I'm working with speakers, they tell a story and make a point, great. Then they might tell another story and make a point, great. Then they might do an activity and make a point, wonderful. All that's tight. It's going to be remembered. But, if they tell a story and make a point and then make three more points, those three additional points will be lost because they're not tied to anything.

What are some examples of anchors?

The four types of anchors I use are: Anecdotes, Activities, Analogies, and Acronyms. For an analogy, I use crabs in a barrel, for example, to be analogous to negative people pulling you down. Every time a crab tries to crawl out, another one will claw it to bring it back down, age-old analogy, right? Anything that can get you to remember the point. It could even be just a picture you have on the screen that gets you to remember a point. If you don't tie it to one of these anchors, then it will not be remembered. That's why when I'm talking to you, I'm using stories to get you to remember.

How do you come up with your stories and what's the best way to tell a story?

I'll give you an example. I was in Los Angeles with my family and we had to get on a plane and leave the next morning. My son was eight and my daughter was ten. My wife says, "Okay, we've got to leave tomorrow, so let's all go to sleep." I said, "I can't go to sleep." She said, "Well, we have to go to sleep because we've got to get up early and get on a flight." I said, "I know, but I can't sleep on demand." My son said, "Well, then sleep on da bed." Now, he's eight years old, so for that to come out was pretty quick. It made us all laugh and I said, "I've got to find a way to turn that into a story."

How do you take an experience and craft it into a story?

Notice what hits you emotionally, and then look for what point it can make. Here's an example. I remember back in 1999, a guy called me and said, "Craig, this is Wade and I'd like you to coach me on public speaking." I said, "Wade, I'm a speaker but I'm not a speech coach. I don't know what to do." He said, "Yeah, but I really want you to coach me." I said, "Wade, I'm not a coach. I wouldn't even know where to start." He said, "I'll pay you." I said, "That's a good place to start." So, I coached him and then I started coaching other people. That's the quick story, but now I've got to look for the point. The point is I fell into speech coaching, but it didn't bring wealth until I jumped into what I fell into. I could then say to my audience, "So jump into what you fall into, because there's a reason you fell and there's a lot of wealth there." I'm looking for what I call a foundational phrase. This is a phrase that is fewer than 10 words and audience focused. It's rhythmic, so it's easy to say, repeatable, and will be remembered. One of my favorite stories and I'm not going to tell it here but the foundational phrase to the story is "Your dream is not for sale."

Yeah, your wife said that, right?

She sure did, so you remember.

Yes.

I gave that story at my store in India and the next morning I woke up and there was a big picture of me on the front cover of the newspaper, but the headline read, "Your dream is definitely not for sale."

Oh, that's cool.

That's when I realized the impact of these foundational phrases. Like I say to people in business, "When you get the buzz, you get the biz," right? When people are buzzing about you, you're going to get more business and that's what gets you that gravitational pull of marketing.

What led to your book, *World Class Speaking in Action*?

When Wade asked me to coach, that started me in coaching. People tell you, you're good at this, so stay in your lane. But, even if you stay in your lane, you have to recognize when the road curves. I was a speaker and that was my lane, but then I realized that people wanted me to coach them, so I started coaching speakers. I stayed in my lane, but I recognized when the road curved. Listen to your market and they will tell you exactly what to create next.

Craig Valentine

How do you manage your time between managing all of these activities and doing keynotes?

It was scary to launch my online Speak and Prosper Academy, because I didn't know if people would sign up. As of last Wednesday, I had twice as many sign-ups as I thought I would. It was tremendously successful, but it was years in the making. Like I say, you invest once and you inspire forever. In terms of managing my time, one of the things that I try to do is write every day. That's the most important thing I can do every day. I write at least 747 words per day and people say why 747? Well, let me ask you, what do you think of if you hear 747? An airplane, right? The more I write, the less I have to fly.

You're so good at coming up with those phrases.

Well, thank you. If I write 747 words per day, then those words turn into products. They turn into teleseminars, courses, and speeches. That's the most important thing I can do in my day. And it keeps me balanced as a business, because if you're just doing keynote speeches and not offering any products or services, it's like having a chair with one leg on it. You're going to be off balance and it will be easy to fall. You have to be balanced with several streams of income and that's what I've been able to do by writing every day.

Along with the writing, how does a speaker create other activities in their business?

You do it by listening to what people say. I recommend you set up two folders. One folder called Attain, and another folder called Avoid. Whenever you're talking to prospects or audience members and they say, "Craig, I'm really worried about this," put it in the Avoid folder. If they say, "Craig, I really would like to do this," put it in the Attain or the Aspire folder. Over time, you'll realize that they're telling you what product to create next.

What's a common problem you see with speakers today?

The most common problem is they retell their stories instead of reliving them. They use way too much narration instead of dialogue. When you use so much narration, it's like a CNN report. When you use too much dialogue, it's like a stage play. So, you need a good mix. Like the story I told you about the salesperson. He said, "Are you looking at that car?" I said, "Yes, sir." He said, "Oh, you're going to look good in that one." He said, "You're going to be flying down the road. The wind is going to be blowing through your hair and the girls, let me tell you, the girls will be all over you." I turn and ask the audience, "What do you think I did?" They reply, "You bought the car." I say, "Absolutely." I turn back and continue, "Where do I sign?" Right? Now, that's a good mix of narration and dialogue. What a lot of speakers do is retell the whole story like, "And the salesperson came over to me and told me that I could probably get more girls if I bought this car. He told me that I looked good in it." You don't want to retell the story. You want them to hear that person's voice and pull them in with dialogue. That's what brings the story to life.

So there's this rhythm of going back and forth between the dialogue, "You're going to look so good in this car," and then addressing the audience, "So, what do you think I said next?"

Exactly. You've got to do some check-ins with the audience, but you hit it right on the head. The secret to storytelling is great dialogue. But, it's the spaces between the lines where the story lives. Just in that story, for example, when he says to me, "You're going to look good in that one," that's an okay line, but when he says, "Oh, you're going to look good in that one," and my face brightens up and I look at the audience like, "Who, me?" Yeah, that's when the story really takes off. It's the spaces and faces between the lines that really make the story work.

It sounds like that's a key piece of connecting with your audience. I've seen you speak and how much you pull them in, almost like you're having a dialogue with them.

That is really the key to master storytelling. Study the art. And I don't mean just study speaking. Study novels. Study screenplays. Study comedians and how you can uncover humor, because I always say never *add* humor, always *uncover* it. When people remember your stories, they're going to remember your points. For example, in 2012 I was watching the Summer Olympics and the oldest person there was a 74-year-old equestrian from Japan. My seven-year-old son and I were watching and all the commentators kept harping on was the guy's age. They kept saying, "He's 74. Can you believe he's 74? By golly, he's 74." Finally, my seven-year-old son looked up and said, "Well, how old is the horse?" It made me laugh. I couldn't get that question out of my mind and that's when I realized my son's question was much more relevant than I thought. My seven-year-old son taught me something important that day about self-development. Never stop asking questions. You see what I did? Something made me laugh, I turned it into a story, looked for the point that it was going to make, and summarized it in a foundational phrase, "Never stop asking questions." People remember that story and the point, and that's what's going to connect us. I also uncovered humor with my son's line. By the way, Maria, that's where you uncover humor, in your stories with your characters, in the dialogue, and in the spaces and faces between the lines.

What do you do when you first walk out on stage?

Before I say anything, I'm sending good thoughts to my audience. I say to myself, "May I forget myself, remember my speech, and touch my audience," because that mindset makes it about them and not me. People can underestimate that but if you don't show up right, your audience is going to see right through you. When I'm walking out on stage, the first thing I do is make sure I'm in that right mindset. Then I jump right into a story or a statement that will make them think, "hmm, this will be different." For example, my first eight or nine years of speaking I would start off like this. The audience would applaud and I'd walk up to the mic and say, "When I was in prison...visiting," with those five words, my audience looked up because they know this was going to be different.

I love that.

In five words, I've got their attention and we're ready to go. I like to start right into a story or a startling statement without thanking people or saying, "I'm so glad to be here." I jump right in and we're off to the races, and then I can thank people who brought me in. It's called the sitcom approach. If you watch any situation comedy nowadays, you'll see that they start the story first and then they go to the opening credits and the opening music because they want to get you hooked in. Right? It's the same with mystery shows. They start with the dead body on the floor, then cut to the opening credits, and then bring you back in, but they want to get you into the story first. That's the same thing we should do on stage.

What a great comparison.

Yeah.

How would you advise someone who is not a full-time speaker but someone who is speaking to build their business?

You must master back of the room sales. By the time you finish your speech, you should have people running to the back to take the exact next step you want them to take. If you're up there speaking and you make a great connection, but there's no next step for them to take, guess what? You missed a perfect opportunity.

What have you learned from setting up speaking gigs and working with events and meeting planners?

When I get booked to speak, I give meeting planners a pre-program questionnaire to fill out so I can find out the pain, and the reason they're bringing me in. Some meeting planners or executives will tell you things they won't write down, so now I try to have conversations with them. Is this the point you want me to make? Do you want me to do it in this way? How am I coming on stage? Who am I introducing? All those things. When you work with them like that, you get rehired. I have an 88% rehire rate, so the more work you can do upfront, the more they're going to rebook you.

And you'll build an ongoing relationship with them.

Right. One of my mentors, said, "Think of the fourth sale first." When you first start working with somebody, you shouldn't just be thinking of just that event, you should be thinking down the line, what more can we do together? Then that relationship is going to spark.

If you could have dinner with anyone, living or not living, who would that be?

I would have to say Frederick Douglass who was probably the most well-known African American in the 1800s. He was my biggest hero in life because he went from being a slave, to being free, to helping other people get free, to being one of the greatest writers in the history of this country, and to moving women's suffrage forward. To me, he was an exceptional person with a life well-lived. If I could have a conversation with someone, that would be the person. And he was a fantastic speaker.

If you knew then what you know now, what would you have done differently?

I would have built my list. When I first started speaking, I should have started gathering names and email addresses because your list is your business. Here's how I learned this. I have a friend named Darren LaCroix who is also a World Champion of Public Speaking back in the day he said, "Craig, you've got to start building your list. Every time you speak, you should have a clipboard and pass it around." He said, "You should give them something in exchange for names and email addresses." This was back in my "I'm an artist" days. I would say, "List, Shmist. I don't need any list. I'm going to give my speech. I'm going to be an artist. And then I'll give another speech." Then he decided to launch this product and he said, "Craig, I'm going to launch my product to my list." I said, "Yeah, yeah, list whatever." Three days later he comes to me and he said, "Craig, I launched my product." I said, "Yeah." He said, "I just made $23,000."

Oh, wow.

I said, "What did you say about this list again?"

Suddenly the list is more interesting.

Back then $23,000 was a lot.

Yeah, it is now, too.

That was when I started building my list. The best thing I did for my list was establishing 52speakingtips.com. What I say to my audiences is, "Raise your hand if a year from now you'd like to be at least three times better than the presenter you are today," and everybody's hands go up. I say, "Great, then for no fee, for free you can go to one of my websites, 52speakingtips.com, and every week for a year, you're going to get an audio lesson from me. At the end of that year you'll be at least three times better than the speaker you are today." People have gone there in droves. Every week they hear from me and that's the way I've built an entire side of my business. Whatever you have, I suggest that you do 52somethingtips.com and offer it for free and build your list.

What a great idea. Craig, this has been so fun and valuable. Thank you for your time today.

You're very welcome. This has been fun to revisit so much of my past and realize the successes along the way.

It's been fun revisiting them with you.

KEY TAKEAWAYS

- Don't sell the product; sell the result.
- Bring your stories to life with a balanced mix of dialogue and narration.
- Tell stories that have a foundational phrase.
- Listen to your market and they will tell you exactly what to create next.
- Master back of the room sales.

ABOUT CRAIG VALENTINE

Craig won Salesperson of the Year for three years for Glencoe/ McGraw-Hill's Mid-Atlantic Division. He became a top-rated award-winning management trainer for one of the most prestigious and largest seminar companies in the U.S., and sold more than $8 million in educational resources in a single year. He also won the Events Manager of the Year for the National Small Business Council, Inc., AND a Congressional Achievement Award from the United States Congress for excellence in communications. He also helped the United Way of Central Maryland reach its $45 million fundraising goal in the year 2000 by training their Loan Executives.

CONTACT

You can find out more about Craig by visiting his website, www.CraigValentine.com where he has a free audio download, "On the Edge of Their Seats." He also has speaking tips, products and services, and a comprehensive blog. Craig is active on social media.

CHAPTER 7:
CYDNEY O'SULLIVAN

"Bad things happen to all of us all the time; it's how we react to them that determines whether we're inspiring to others."
-Cydney O'Sullivan

Cydney O'Sullivan is the founder of Millionaires Academy and Motivational Speakers International in Sydney, Australia. An international best-selling author and publishing consultant, she's helped hundreds of people thrive with fast, results-oriented solutions to success. After a successful career in real estate investing, Cydney answered her calling to help others reach their full potential and build wealth in their lives. She has created a profitable speaking, publishing and mentoring practice.

Welcome, Cydney.

Thank you so much for including me in this fantastic project, Maria. Lovely to be here with you.

Take us back to the beginning. Why did you want to become a speaker?

When I was little girl I had big dreams, but I was very shy. I came across an opportunity to be in a school play and it changed everything for me. I really came out of my shell and loved being in school plays, singing, and being on stage.

You said you were shy as a young girl, but then you dove into these school plays. How did you gain the confidence to do that?

When we get on stage as speakers, we're sometimes afraid that they're not going to like us. Or, we think we're not good enough, so we get choked up and nervous. When you're acting, they're not judging *you*, because you're pretending to be somebody else. You become a different character and you're able to get out of your own way. Whenever I'm speaking on stage, I remember that I'm there to be of value to the audience. It's not about me, it's about them. Just like acting, once you take the focus off you, you don't worry as much about being judged.

You eventually moved into business. How did you build your practice?

When I was a young adult, I moved to LA where it was a lot more competitive. I stopped speaking and acting for a while, and started buying and restoring run-down businesses and then selling them. My husband and I did that several times and we became millionaires at quite a young age.

What was that like for you?

We had come into all this wealth and I found myself thinking, "Why do I still feel so unfulfilled?" One day, I attended a self-development seminar and watched a lady taking hundreds of people through these personal breakthroughs. I thought, "Wow, I want do that. I want to be back up on stage changing people's lives." That's when I got back into speaking.

That's exciting. You got the bug again.

Yeah. But then I had to learn *how* because it's not like you can just say, "I want to be on stage," and be a good speaker, right? You need some training. So, I started taking speaker courses. As I was going to these, I told them I wanted to be a speaker and they would give me opportunities. They would say, "Hey, do you want to do the breakout session," or, "Would you like to come speak at our event for a little while?" Doing that allows you to keep working on your speaking skills until you're good at it, which is what *you* help people with.

How did your speaking start to grow after that?

After I started writing books and speaking about them, I found people were *way* more interested in learning how I got my books done than they were in hearing about my business success, or even the content in the books! People were always saying, "I want to write a book, how did you get that book written? How did you get it published? How did you get it promoted?

Sounds like there's a big market for that.

They say that 80% of people out there have an idea for a book, but don't know how to get it executed. This is what I've done for 10 or 12 years. I show people how to get their books written, published, and promoted. I speak around many different marketing topics, like social media, marketing, PR and media. If you're talking from your heart and really know your topic, it's pretty easy to get speaking opportunities. Especially these days with so many networking events and meetups. There are so many groups putting on events. They're always looking for speakers to bring high value that will help their business clients.

When you speak, what's the first thing you do to engage the group?

One of the most powerful things is to have a great introductory video, and I don't see enough speakers doing this. It's really powerful if you take the time to craft a video that sets you up as the expert from the very beginning of your presentation. A great sizzle reel that has a little bit about your background, and some great music, can set the whole mood of the room. It sets you up as the authority right from the start.

Storytelling is such a big piece of speaking. How do you pull in stories throughout?

Stories are magical. I like using real stories about real clients or successes that I've had. If I'm doing a motivational talk, people want to hear my story because I've had a lot of ups and downs. I went through cancer last year and all my speaker clients were saying, "Chin up, you're going to have a great story at the end of this." It was a big breakthrough for me when they gave me the cancer diagnosis. I thought, "How am I going to tell my kids that I have cancer?" Everything changed for me. Suddenly, all my priorities shifted. I made the decision right there at the doctor's office, "Well, I could look at this as a life sentence or I can look at this as an opportunity for a life makeover." It changed my entire reaction to my cancer, and it actually became the best thing that ever happened to me.

What changed after that?

Everything changed. I had better connection with my clients, I got more focused and decided who I wanted to work with. If you've had turning points in your life where you came to a fork in the road, and you could've taken one path leading to a particular outcome, but you chose the *other* path, what did that do for your life? People like to hear these stories. It has to be a story that they can relate to, that they can see themselves in.

Well, first of all, I'm very glad to hear that you're healthy.

Thank you. Since I got all clear with my cancer, I've gone back to work from a place of wanting to serve. I actually start my speeches with, "Thank you for letting me be here. I'm here to deliver as much value as I can in the time we have, and I mean it." And, if you truly want to move people, they *feel* it. What's amazing is that now I attract the people I want to work with. When I speak from the heart, even when I have to tell them some tough love, I attract fabulous clients with whom I can connect on a deep level, like a love affair. The more authentic you can be, the more connected you are with that audience, and the more you're going to attract the right kind of people into your life.

How did you become interested in booking speakers?

I was always going to seminars and meeting speakers, and the common problem I kept hearing was, "Gosh, I would love to get more speaking opportunities." So, I started helping a few clients with their marketing. I noticed that many had not spent enough time building their personal brand. Be sure you build a speaker profile online that's strong, credible, and positions you as the speaker that people want to bring to their events.

How did you figure out that online branding was the issue?

I was having trouble getting bookings for clients because event organizers would Google them and say, "I'm not finding enough information about this person as a speaker." That's still a problem today, because the Google landscape is always changing so you must be proactive about it. You have to keep putting stuff out there to position yourself. Event organizers want you to be a big enough name to fill events and make attendees excited to come.

That's when you started your speaking bureau.

Yes. I started Motivational Speakers International and I've been helping clients build their speaking profile by putting them on our websites. As a bureau, we pass gigs around that come in through the websites and recommend speakers for gigs. We put them in books and promote the books out to the industry. We also have training to help them understand how to build their star brand. Because, after six months off for my cancer treatment, I found when I came back to work, my brand was better than money in the bank. I was able to re-launch bigger, faster, and stronger as soon as I put the word out that I wanted to get back out there, because I had built that personal brand.

How does somebody do that? You mentioned Google. What else should people should be doing?

One of the most important things you can do is write a book in your area of expertise. It doesn't have to be a big book but it's one of the fastest ways that you can build your credibility. It shows people you know your topic and it showcases your expertise. Nowadays, it's faster and easier to write a book and get it published than ever before. We used to have to get publishers to accept our books. Now, we can publish straight on to Amazon, which is the hundred-pound gorilla on the internet these days.

What advice do you have for people wanting to write a book?

You can write a book as little as 50 or 100 pages. Make sure it represents you well, and put the effort into making it a good, professional book. Because, this is going to be a marketing tool that will position you as the expert. You'll also get so much clarity in your message from writing the book. Then, you get a publisher, someone like me, to help you. Or there are plenty of other publishers to help you on Amazon or other platforms. Make sure it's the topic you want to get booked for as a speaker, because an unrelated novel isn't going to help you build your speaking brand. Start posting videos on your topic of expertise on a regular basis, on YouTube, Facebook, or Instagram. This will start building up your Google profile. It's great practice, great exposure, and a great way to expand your reach.

How else can a book help you?

Take that content you created in the book and turn it into training programs. Really, there are so many platforms for doing these easily and promoting your online trainings that are begging for content. There are not enough speakers who are doing this.

You've really got this down.

I actually have a formula, I wrote a book about it. I call it my STARS formula. You might find this helpful. Figure out what your strengths are, what your message is, and what you want to speak about. Here's the "S." Don't worry about what you're not good at, because that'll just hold you back. Focus on your strengths and where you're already getting traction. The "T" is to find your tribe. Who do you want to attract, work with, and have strategic alliances with? That's your tribe. Start establishing your authority. That's the "A." We talked about how you do videos and write a book. Amazon will get you great Google love and there's also LinkedIn. LinkedIn is linked to Google, so you want to start building up your authority profile on LinkedIn because that'll be one of the first things that comes up on Google for you. Remember to talk about your speaking there because a lot of people forget that. The "R" is for reach. Begin using these tools to expand your reach to new audiences. The last "S" is for scale. Start putting in systems. That's my formula.

That's great and easy to remember.

Because we're stars, right?

For someone who's starting and doesn't have a lot of videos yet, how can you start this?

If you're at a monthly networking meeting, you can have someone take a picture of you standing in front of the group. Or, record some testimonials on your phone from people talking about you speaking. You can record yourself in your own home initially just to practice. It's a good idea to record your speeches and listen back to them. If more speakers did this, they would probably be better speakers. Record yourself on video or audio, and just listen to it again and again. How can I fix that, how can I improve that, what do I need, do I need voice training?

What should people keep in mind when they're making calls to organizations or looking up meeting planners to get a gig?

You need to have a professional speakers kit. I see way too many speakers who don't have this. A nice one-sheet, and these are pretty important in America. We don't use them as much in Australia but it's still a great thing to have. For a one-sheet, include relevant information about you, your book, your topic, and a picture of you. That information needs to fit onto one sheet so that event planners have everything they need in a concise format. You can also have a video of you presenting or an audio they can listen to in the car. Then start sending it out and you may have to send it out a lot. What's great now is you can do it digitally which means you're not having to spend a lot of money on mailing, unless they ask for it by mail. You also want to have a one-sheet for the media, so you can get out to media as well, which also helps build your brand.

How do you go about getting media?

There are websites like RTIR, for instance, Radio-Television Interview Reporter where journalists are looking for people to interview for different stories. I think it comes out a couple of times a day and you can volunteer to do media interviews. Relationships count. When they come to a website like mine, or any of the bureau sites, they're going to be faced with hundreds of speakers to choose from. That's long and hard work for event managers. Start building your relationship with them and getting in front of them. Go to industry events and pay to be a sponsor. And have a professional speakers kit that you can send them.

You mentioned sponsorship. What would you say about that?

It's a great way to get in front of your target market. Look for expos and events, networking events, Chambers of Commerce, or community events where they have your audience. There are events going on anywhere from, say, 50 people meeting on a regular basis to thousands of people who could be your target market. That comes from knowing your tribe. A lot of events and expos have sponsorship packs available. You can say, "Would you like me to come on as a sponsor? I'll be happy to put some money towards the event if you let me have some time on your stage," and they'll love you for it a lot of the time. If they don't offer stage time, ask if you can do a breakout or lunch session.

Great advice. What's your advice for people who are just beginning to get booked at events?

If you're doing a talk or breakout at an event, attending the entire event is key. I go to the whole event even if I'm only there to speak for an hour, so I understand the mood in the room and what the other speakers are saying. Then I can tailor my speech appropriately. A lot of speakers just blow in and blow out. I've seen more speakers make mistakes with their presentations because they didn't understand the audience or the feel of the event because they didn't come early. They miss the chance to make a connection with the audience AND the event organizer.

That's a great idea.

When you're there, you can jump in and fill spots when there's a problem with the scheduling, say if someone ends too early and they have 20 minutes to fill. Be willing to get up there and be that person for them. That really endears you to the event host. A lot of times they're not thinking about their next events, so you can say, "Hey, if you like what I did for you at this event and you have other events, I could help you with them." Then they'll say, "Oh yeah, we do have other events." Always think about how you can get repeat bookings and how you can be of service.

That's helpful. Cydney, who do you admire as a speaker?

Who do I admire? Wow. Well, I love people who can be super funny on stage. When someone comes out and they have the skill to be funny or moving, it's a gift, really, to the audience because it gives them a break. They get to have a laugh, they get to feel. I think if you're going to build your skills as a speaker, look to people who found a way of making the audience laugh. Maybe do a stand-up or improv course so that you can learn to make people laugh if you think you're naturally funny. Or watch some of the great motivational speakers. I love to watch Tony Robbins, I think he's fantastic. I love to listen to Brian Tracy. I listen in the car all the time. I love Jim Rohn's stuff.

How can somebody use the stage and their voice to be more impactful in their speaking?

Don't stand behind the lectern. Get in the habit of moving around, but not too much. You must have this balance between waving your hands around to the point where it's annoying, and using your hands with purpose. Study body language because there are gestures that relay messages on a subconscious level. Some gestures will make people more likely to trust you, and others will actually alienate them. You know how they say if you scratch your nose, you're probably lying? That's one example.

Yeah, like having your palms facing out.

Exactly, that's a trust gesture. Having your hands out and open, palms facing the audience, and your arms open, is like a mother position. On a subconscious level, you're going to get the audience leaning in more when you have these kinds of gestures. It takes some time to learn how to use your body with volition and purpose. Some speakers believe when you're talking about negative things, you should be on the left side of the stage. When you're talking about positive things, you're on the right side. If you're just starting out, focus first on knowing your speech really well, so you don't have to read it off the slides.

This is excellent information.

I work with a lot of speakers. I help a lot of speakers get booked. And I can tell you the things they are doing wrong. They have not built their personal brand, they don't have a professional speakers kit, and they don't go into an event realizing that they can be a great asset to the event host. Do not be a diva and cause a lot of trouble for the event host. They have enough to deal with without their speakers showing up late, not communicating, not sending them their videos in time. Speakers can do this kind of stuff and it's very disrespectful. And then they wonder why they don't get another booking.

You've been through so many experiences for years in different aspects of publishing, speaking and business. Looking back at everything, what has surprised you the most?

I should have been doing this years ago. I should have gotten over my own fears of being judged, because I could have been changing so many more lives. I could have been living into my destiny and my purpose in life so much earlier. If you're a person who is thinking you would like to be a speaker, but you think maybe you're not good enough, do it anyway. Get out of your own way and do it anyway. You are enough. You're more than enough.

Any last words of advice?

When I first started writing my first book, I was very successful in business already, and had a great idea for a book. Because I was working with great mentors like Jack Canfield and Mark Victor Hansen, they introduced me to a literary agent who had literally just gotten Eckhart Tolle on Oprah. He was looking for more people to put on Oprah and he just said, "Hey, let's get this book finished, let's get you on Oprah." My insecurities and self-sabotage kicked in and I never went ahead with it. This was my dream, to get on Oprah. We do this to ourselves all the time because we don't think we're good enough. My mantra now is act successful and then become successful. Act as if it's already happened and it will happen.

I love that. Just allow it to happen, step into it.

The more you connect with your network out a spirit of service, the more they're likely to give back. This is a tricky thing because when you have a large network like a lot of us do, and you become a speaker where people want something from you all the time, you have what's called the halo effect. You come on stage, people feel like they really know you because you've been up there for an hour telling your story. Still, you have to protect your energy and your time because you can't give everything of yourself away to everyone. One challenge is that people always want to get access to your network. I do believe you should still be as generous as possible with your network, while still thinking of ways you can be paid for your time and energy. It's a balance.

I've heard of other people getting into a protective energy space before they go on to speak. Do you have anything that you do before you go on?

I do a grounding exercise because I still get nervous. Before I go on stage, I stand like a tree, really try to get grounded and remember that I'm there to give inspiration and value, to teach. I want to make sure that I don't talk too fast, and that I talk from a lower register. Being a woman, we have to be careful to not start talking too high pitched. I do an exercise where I talk from my lower diaphragm, projecting from a lower octave. If I start in a lower octave, then I'm more likely to stay there through the rest of the speech. I just try to get really grounded with the earth so that I'm coming from a position of feeling empowered, not on the back foot, if that makes sense.

Yup, not on your heels but leaning forward.

Yeah. Then I'll also try to channel from above, from the universe. I'll say, "Whatever I'm supposed to deliver, whoever out here I'm supposed to touch and move, let it happen." I try to connect beneath and above.

What a great image.

That's when you come from a high, authentic, connected place.

That's wonderful. Thank you so much for sharing all of this. It's going to provide so much value and help others move forward.

Thank you, Maria. I'm so excited about this because you're going to help so many people with this book. There are hundreds and hundreds of people out there who want to be speakers. You grow as a person by putting yourself up there in front of those audiences. It's a magical thing to step into. I'm sure you have heard plenty of times that people fear public speaking more than death. What a terrible thing to be going around in life worrying about getting up and doing a speech. It's a gift to get over that.

It's amazing, isn't it? And, so many people need to do it as part of their work.

Yeah. Get over that, just learn to enjoy it. Learn to love it.

Wonderful. Thank you so much for your time, Cydney.

Thank you so much, Maria.

KEY TAKEAWAYS:

▸ Have an introductory sizzle reel that sets the mood.

▸ Attend the entire event, and be prepared to present on request if needed.

▸ Build a strong, credible speaker profile online.

▸ Create a professional speakers kit with a one-sheet.

▸ Go to industry events and pay to become a sponsor.

ABOUT CYDNEY O'SULLIVAN

Cydney has trained with some of the world's most successful business mentors including Brian Tracy, Jay Conrad Levinson and Jack Welch. Many are now part of the roster of international speakers she represents.

CONTACT:

You can learn more about Cydney at www.MillionairesAcademy.com, where you'll have access to free training from successful speakers, as well as the opportunity to receive some of her books for free. You can access www.MotivationalSpeakersInternational.com and find Cydney and many other speakers listed. Cydney is also on social media.

CHAPTER 8:
JANIE JASIN

"I listen to people, that's where the miracles are."
-Janie Jasin

 Janie is a speaker, author, humorist, and storyteller. She's been a successful professional speaker for 40 years. In the 1970s, Janie was in sales for Dale Carnegie training, and then formed her own corporation in 1976. She's an author, and her bestselling book, *The Littlest Christmas Tree,* sold two million copies. Janie holds the Certified Speaking Professional (CSP) designation in the National Speakers Association that only 10% of all speakers receive. In 2012, Janie received the coveted Lifetime Achievement Award from the National Speakers Association, and is a 2015 Legends of Speaking Award Winner.

Welcome Janie, it's great having you here.

Thank you so much. I'm all yours.

Let's go back in time a little bit and share with us, how did it all begin? What's your story?

I'm the product of two grandparents who were Irish musicians in Wisconsin, so as a little girl, I saw a lot of dancing and playing. In the olden days, the polio epidemic was horrendous. I started putting on little shows in the garage and collecting money for charity. For me, it was always about, "let's do a show." That all was very normal to me. I'm also an only child, and I had a father who was an entrepreneur who encouraged me.

Many people have difficulty with this aspect of speaking. What are the keys to being a good storyteller?

I listen to people, that's where the miracles are. I'm not so interested in myself anymore because I've had a phenomenal life. To give a good story, you need to stand up and say something. Give me some hope. Give me a kernel of strength. Give me something I can laugh at. Those stories are spectacular. We get preoccupied with the things we do. We count the money, or we drive the truck, or we bake at the bakery, and we stop looking at what's going on around us. That's where the magic is. If you have the nerve, the guts, the interest, or the love of wanting to speak, then the sky is the limit and you can stand up and talk about almost anything. Wake people up to do their best around you.

Where do you find your material?

It is about using what you have or what's current in the day. I always try to use what was a current song or whatever I have. I remember working at Dale Carnegie in sales. Oh, I was so proud of that. I was the only woman on that sales team. One day a man said, "Well, would you get me coffee?" I stood up, and I just stuck my bosoms out as big as I could and I said, "Nope. I'm a salesman."

What was it like when your book came out?

When *The Littlest Christmas Tree* came out, I really didn't know anything about book sales, and how all of that worked. I was excited about the crowds that were coming, and at the book expo there was a big pile of people standing in line. I didn't know why and I said, "What are you waiting for?" They said, "We're waiting for the Christmas tree lady." I said, "Well, I'm her," but this crowd was like an audience. I said, "Well, let's learn the song that I wrote." Oh, it was a big crowd of 150 people. I sang and said, "Sing it back." Oh, they sang, and they sang the whole song line after line. And guess who was walking by at that very moment? A CNN reporter, and she covered the whole story!

Oh, my gosh.

CNN did a huge writeup of "The Littlest Christmas Tree" and the book was not about Santa or reindeer. It was about growing and going on. It was about the little tree that needed to learn patience. She stood in the field, and said, "Thank you for allowing me to grow today and to see the world and it's many possibilities."

Is the Littlest Christmas Tree you?

I suppose she was like me. She was a tree I found in a big Christmas tree field in Wisconsin, while I was crying in the forest, because my both parents had lost their minds. I was there trying to deal with their estate. I'm an only child, so I was crying. I thought, "I'll just walk in the Christmas trees," and their soil was so warm, and the branches of the big trees were rubbing me. They seemed like guardian angels and then I looked over, and there was this one little tree on the side, and I thought, "I don't know if that one's going to make it." So, that Christmas, I wrote the story on one page, and sent it to my speaking clients.

So, what happened?

My wonderful career and the speaking was all put on hold. I was dealing with my mom and dad, and that's why I wrote that to my clients. But, there was a power greater than me that had a different plan. I wrote the story with the love I have for life and would wish that love for you, too. That's all any of us can hope for. That's what you're doing, Maria. You're helping people be able to stand up and say something. It's strange that people are so frightened of speaking when it is the first thing we try to do as little babies.

You have such compassion. When you speak, it's not at all about you.

Oh, but it is. They clap for me. I love that, and they turn the lights on, and they play music. I want everybody to have a good time. Okay. Stand up. It's just so great.

Do you invent things on the spot?

I sometimes invent things in the agenda, in the speech. There's always the opening, middle, and a close, and I like to do creative things within that using music, movement, and art. That is the fun of it. You can teach and encourage people using that.

You mentioned you had a beginning, middle, and end. When you first walk out, what's the very first thing you do?

Pray. I look at them, and I say, "Please, God, help me." I'm usually right down by the people within a couple minutes. I move up and down the aisles and stand on the platform when doing big parts of the talk.

On the floor with them?

Oh, yes. I'm starting out with whatever the opener is, "Today we're going to be talking about enthusiasm. What does that mean? Who has it? There are some who don't have it. Some people came here needing it." Bam. Down I go to steps one, two, three, four. I see a man smiling and say, "You, sir, you look like you're a very enthusiastic person." I'm into the people. The minute you walk into them, you ask them, "Oh, was it hard to get up this early? Oh, yeah. You brought your husband? I thought it was only for women. Oh, you're here, sir? When did you meet her?" Now I'm into their life. "You met her where, at a dance, did you? I suppose you got up early this morning, and didn't even have time to kiss her, did you, before this conference began? Where did you meet her? Oh, you met her at a dance. Let's sing. Everybody sing with me." May I have this dance for the rest of my life- (singing) and they do...

You make such great connections with the audience.

I'm always looking for a way to connect with them in a mini moment, because I have the content of the talk. I'm hired to come to deliver a sense of purpose, a sense of well-being and a sense of humor, and I need to make sure people can get them. In between, they are going to experience it, and then I can talk to them, and allow them to be seated and enjoy each other. When the speech is over, they're out in the hallway, and they're all talking. "Oh, I saw you up in front. Janie had you up there, and then you danced." They just love it, so they're the stars and I am the facilitator.

How did you get so good at that?

I didn't always have that ability to connect and wasn't very connected to my own feelings. But after working on it for years, it's like the song Amazing Grace. I once was lost but now I'm found, was blind but now I see. It's all about amazing grace.

What is the hardest part of speaking that you think looks easy to people on the outside?

I think the hardest part is the prep, for me, in the office. What is it going to be? What parts am I going to use, so I draw circles with possibilities. Then in the end, I put the circles in a line, or I choose three out of five, and I put it together like that. When I get to the event, the hardest thing is being nice, because there are always things that are wrong. I don't want a lectern. I just need a chair up here, and the steps going down the middle. Do you have the sound tuned in? Are the lights up? Is the microphone working? Is the book signing area prepped so they see it as they enter the seating area?

What's a memorable experience you can remember speaking about your book?

I went to the Minnesota Zoo when the Christmas book came out, they were going to have me read it in the evening. I went in this room and there were people there that had been touring the zoo.

While I'm getting ready to go on, a woman comes in, and she has her daughter, and the daughter has a red and white cane. The girl is blind, so I say to her, "Well, how do *you* check for buying a Christmas tree?" She said, "I lean into it and I feel the branches." When I saw the little girl, my first thought was, "Well, how is she going to see these people acting out the tree story? So, I'll just put her in." So now in my mind, I had the plan. I'm going to have some people, seniors over 60, be the tall trees. I'm going to put them up on the platform. I'm going to have some little ones that are the little trees. And I'm going to lead the trimmers into the story. Trim the trees, stand up, look good. Then I said to this little blind girl, "At the end, I want you to be standing behind one of the bigger, tall people, as if you're checking the tree." She said, "Okay. Okay." Now the story starts out. Once upon a time in a field, da, da, da. We're going along. We're doing well. All the little children, they're up, they're down, and they're all around, and then, the lights go out in the Minnesota Zoo. Not planned. Dark.

Oh, my gosh.

I know the story, so I just kept going and they kept acting it out. There was kind of a dim hall light or something and then the last line came. "At last, the Littlest Christmas Tree understood the magic was in today." At that very moment, the lights came on in the Minnesota Zoo, and that girl, Annessa, was reaching up on the big tree and looking up, and I said, "She understood that the magic was today. Looking up, she said, 'Thank you for life, thank you for dreams, and thank you for choosing me to grow today in this world with its many possibilities.'" Bam. It was done.

Wow. That is just amazing. That's beyond coincidence

I had to think of something. Yeah. Big stuff happens, but that's the risk. I didn't want to drag my stuff into the Minnesota Zoo, my little bestselling books, and when the light goes out I just sit back at a card table and say, "Well, sorry, folks. "Time's up. Go home." By gosh, we're just going to do it.

What motivates you to do this?

The truth is, I have a drive that's so strong to help other speakers experience the best of themselves. If you have the nerve, the guts, the interest, or the love of wanting to speak, then the sky is the limit. You can stand up at showers, weddings, your church, or anywhere. You can do almost anything, and awaken people to do their best around you. I just get very excited about speaking. I guess I will always be excited that somebody can stand up and say something, and try to make a difference in somebody's life. What a miracle.

What's the worst thing that's happened to you as a speaker?

Once, the guy speaking before me was using technology and the stage was full of it. I was supposed to go on at 10:00 and speak for 90 minutes. However, he ran a half-hour over. I knew that I was supposed to end at 11:30. However, I didn't get on until 10:30, so I decided to end it at 11:30 to be on time. The meeting planning woman, God bless her, was so upset, and she started screaming, "You cheated us. You cheated us." She was afraid she would get reprimanded. She was sitting at her lunch table and I just gave the check back. It was hard.

What was the hardest part about speaking at that time in your life?

The hard parts were the travel and sometimes the loneliness. Sometimes I would go to the hotel room and not want to go in anymore, and I would just have to pray and say, "It's okay, Janie. You just sleep now, and then in the morning, you're out of this room, and then you're speaking, which you love to do. That's where the wear and tear was.

You've worked with a lot of great speakers. Who were some of your mentors?

Jack Canfield was always great to me. Zig Ziglar and Og Mandino were very kind. Cavett Robert sent me cassettes when I started. He was just great to me. Then the support of the National Speakers Association cheered me on. I remember I was going to speak at an event and Jack Canfield spoke before me. I was waiting in line for dinner the night before, and the people in line were just shouting, "Oh, Jack. He's so wonderful. Jaaack. Do you know Jaaack?" The next morning, I was going to be on, and Jack was at the panel's breakfast table behind me. I get up there, and want to get even, so I say to the audience, "Well, here we are, and I'm up here with Jaaack." I look over at Jack. I say, "Wow, they just couldn't say enough wonderful things about you, Jaaack." He was laughing so hard. I said, "Yes, yes, and now I'm up here with him. I don't know who you were last night when we were getting ready for dinner, but I know you wanted to be near Jack. Here he is. Stand up and give him a standing ovation," so they did.

What a great story. Janie, if you could have dinner with anyone living or not living, who would that be?

Cavett Robert.

Why?

He was an attorney from the South, and ended up moving to Arizona. He was in sales, and decided to ask his friends to meet at the Camelback Inn in Arizona and start a group, and that's how The National Speakers Association began. Who knew that six or seven men would turn out to be what, 2,500 people, and this association would begin. The fact that you or I could like this speaking stuff and be doing it as an occupation, a vocation, is a gift.

After all these years, what do you think needs to change?

It would be great if people would encourage presenters to use emotion and not just share the facts. For example, I worked for General Mills and that's the home of Betty Crocker. They chose Betty for her warm and friendly sound, and Crocker was the name of one of the first CEOs. Betty was a name during the war.

Betty was making things from scratch. That's what it was about, warming the visitors, warming the customers to purchase something that would be good for their family. Nothing says loving like something from the oven. It helps when businesses are less about facts and slides, and more about emotion.

I love that.

I think that I've been extremely blessed to meet you, because it awakened me to all this great stuff that occurred in my life, and I'm selfish enough that I want some more stuff.

I don't see you as selfish.

Oh, I am. I just stagger around and think, "Okay, how can I use this now? How do you learn to do this speaking thing?"

After all these years, all the things that you've done, what has surprised you the most?

The surprise was being pulled out of the speaking and having to deal with my mother and father, and being in the Christmas trees, desperately searching for something to write to all of these companies that hired me, and to write them that little story about the Christmas tree on one page. I just did that because I had to send them something. I was pulled out of my work, out of marketing, and out of the speaking world. At that very time, the one page story was sent to Vicky Lansky, a publisher, and she saw that, and said, "I think we should do that. I think we should publish," and I was so naïve. I never saw myself as any kind of a real author. I was just writing to people because I cared about them. The fact that that happened, that was a surprise.

What was it like having that published?

The truth was I really didn't know anything about publishing. Looking back I think, "Oh, my. The publisher really did a lot of work." Then it happened a second time with a piece of music that I wrote for it, and then I did it a third time with the stories of

Annessa, the little girl at the zoo, and some babies in their
incubators. A lot of mileage came out of that, and a play, we
wrote a play that could be done in schools and churches, where
they acted it out. It was pretty much of a miracle.

**What advice do you have for other people out there who are on
this path, and just getting out there?**

I don't think you can go wrong joining the National Speakers
Association. As you book places to speak, one place will
recommend the other place, and that's where the best stuff comes
from. Not from your website, or your ad, or your book.
Somebody knows somebody, so what happens is the meeting
planner is sitting there with the committee. "Who are we going to
get? Oh, did you see the video? Yes, I did. I saw the video." Then,
somebody walks in the door, and they say, "I just saw the greatest
speaker," and they all go, "Well, who was it? Can we get her?"

**How does somebody who is speaking for free move into being
a paid speaker?**

Start by looking at some places that you've felt comfortable
approaching in the past, whether it was a long-term care center, a
church, etc. Work with people you know. Like "Mary Smith."
She's in charge of the women's program. You would say, "Mary,
this is Janie Jasin. I'm working on a wonderful talk about saints
and sinners." Just making this up, "and I understand you have a
women's group." Mary says, "Yes, we do." Then she says, "Is
there a fee?" I would say, "I do have a fee of $1,500." She says,
"Oh, we'd have to pay that much?" "However, I could do an
honorarium for $500, and I would be glad to throw in the travel
costs. It's reframing. You start with the number, and then you
back off to an honorarium number, but you never say, "I go for
free."

**Some people work speaking for free in a different way to get
value out of it. Many places allow you to either give out a free
gift and collect people's information. You can mention**

something about your program, and end up getting leads or referrals.

I don't think I ever spoke for free unless it was for a donation situation. But I have been to some women's networking groups like that. There is also Rotary and Chamber of Commerce.

Earlier, I heard you talk about doing some coaching around books and book launches.

Yes. There are definitely ways to manage and sell your books at a book launch. The books should be set up at the outset. Just like people passing by and buying popcorn before the movie, books need to be seen and purchased before entering the room. It is powerful as a tool for authors who don't want to see their book stored forever in the garage. Many of my colleagues presell and sign their books for the attendees before the conference.

How did you start to raise your prices?

By 1983, somebody said, "You know, Janie's pretty good. She might be good for the NSA noon luncheon in Las Vegas." When I came out of the talk, a meeting planner was standing there, and he said, "How much do you charge?" I said, "Well, like $500." He said, "You better quadruple your fee." But at that time, I was too scared to do that. Later, a team of people was planning the National Speakers Association summer convention in Washington, D.C., and somebody said, "We should have Janie as the luncheon speaker." Man, I cranked it out there. And after that it was $2,500, then $3,000, and eventually up to $10,000. Bam, bam, bam. That's when it took off. It was a miracle.

That's awesome. How did you become comfortable with that over time?

The wonderful NSA pioneers, including Cavett, and Og Mandino, Patricia Fripp, and a lot of these people said, "You're really good." It was a combination of using business savvy, emotions, humor and praise for other people, along with pride for our country and the freedom in life. My programs ended with the American flag and the audience singing, "Oh, beautiful for spacious skies." They were all standing. This was the kickoff for my 1985 speech launching into miracles.

Looking back, if you knew then what you know now, what would you have done differently?

I would've relaxed and realized that I had been given amazing talent, and that God was working with me.

This has been amazing talking with you, Janie. Thank you so much for your time today.

You are so welcome. It was a blessing for me to recollect and be grateful for all these exquisite experiences that I've had, and to connect with the next generation that can pass it on. I send my prayers, my love, and my encouragement. People need to hear you, learn from you and what your journey is about. It will help them on their journey. Thank you. God bless you.

KEY TAKEAWAYS

- Listen to people, that's where the miracles are.
- Join the National Speakers Association.
- If you have the nerve and love of speaking, then the sky's the limit.
- Use emotion and don't just share the facts.
- People need to hear your journey, because it will help them on their journey.

ABOUT JANIE JASIN

In 2015, Janie received the Legends Award from the Veterans Speakers Association in Washington, D.C. She's been a guest speaker on PBS, and in 2004, her life story was featured on a major news network. In 1992, she was presented the Educational Achievement Award from the National Nursing Home

Educators, and in 2001, she received the Governor's Award for her contribution to the citizens of Wisconsin. She continues teaching and delighting her audiences and speaking students.

> ## CONNECT
>
> You can learn more about Janie through her website www.janiespeaks.com, where she has many videos, products and a blog. She also now has an app that you can download for free from the app store. It's called "The Talker. Janie Jasin." Janie's accessible by phone, email, Facebook and LinkedIn.

CHAPTER 9:
CHRISTY WHITMAN

"When you take yourself out of the equation, you can come from a totally different perspective."
-Christy Whitman

Christy Whitman is a transformational leader, abundance coach, speaker, and the New York Times bestselling author of, "The Art of Having It All." She has appeared on *The Today Show* and *The Morning Show*, and her work has been featured in *People Magazine, Seventeen* and *Woman's Day*. Christy is the founder of the Quantum Success Learning Academy, and Quantum Success Coaching Academy, a 12-month transforming coaching certification program. Christy has helped hundreds of thousands of people worldwide to achieve their goals through her empowerment seminars, speeches and coaching sessions and products.

Thanks so much for joining us. Welcome, Christy.

Thank you so much, Maria. I'm thrilled that you asked me, so it's great to be here.

Could you share with us how you got into speaking?

I became a seeker of spiritual knowledge about 20 years ago, and started working with the universal laws when nothing in my life was working. About five years into learning the laws and applying them, I began seeing amazing results in my life. Things like coming into my ideal body, getting out debt, getting married to a wonderful man. Literally, everything in life changed. I had a book that came to me in a meditation in the middle of the night, and I became an author. I started speaking in spiritual bookstores and churches. That's how I started my speaking career.

What was your first big speaking gig like?

I was really nervous, but I knew the information, the order in which I was speaking, and the points I was making. That made me feel a lot calmer and more secure. Still, speaking in front of 200 people, which was more than I'd spoken to before was a lot of pressure. There were many people in the room that I really admired, people that I had learned from. I thought, "Oh my gosh. I have to do really well." That first time, I put a lot of pressure on myself, so much so that my personality really didn't come out as it does now. I'm much more relaxed now. I was a bit scared and insecure with the lights on me. But, as I practiced and honed my message, and became more comfortable in my own skin, it has become easier.

You can get so intimate and deep with people, and at the same time, you're bubbly and down to earth. How do you do that?

I got to know myself and connected more with the divine inside of me. I healed and didn't feel like I needed to please others in order to be loved. I felt more comfortable in my own skin and with what I was teaching. That brought me more confidence.

How do you stay connected to your authentic self?

I always check in with myself to make sure that I'm staying true to my message and what's true for me. What's important to me is being in alignment with my divinity, and that is my authenticity. Nobody else is like me. Nobody else has my story. Nobody else has the same conditioning, programming, successes, and failures.

There is only one unique me. Others might be sharing similar information, such as law of attraction coaches. Some people say, "Why are you doing that [teaching coaches]? It's like creating your own competition." I come from the perspective that nobody is really my competition. The people who resonate with me are going to want to learn from me, and they are going to be best served by me being true to who I am. I'm the only person that understands the universal laws from my perspective, that has my particular stories, in my words. Others may use the same exact words that I use, but for them, it's not authentic. And if they are not authentic, they're not going to be as successful.

Let's talk a little bit about QSCA, Quantum Success Coaching Academy. What led you to creating it? How did it change you?

I had the idea planted in my head to do a law of attraction certification program, and I said to myself, "I'm a coach but I don't certify people, right?" So, the idea came in, and I dismissed it. And then I met a woman who was doing her own certification with her brand. She was doing really well and doing a lot of good. I just took in that information, and then within four days, I had four different people ask me to certify them. The first person was a client I had on a Monday, and she was really adamant. I had this argument with her kind of like, "I don't do that." The next night in Montreal, I had a woman in my 2-day abundance training come up to me and say, "I wanna learn to do what you do. Do you certify people to do what you do?" And I said, "No, I don't but I could send you where I got certified." The second night of the series, a man walked up to me and said, "Okay, so I would love to do what you do. Can you certify me to do what you do?" I'm like, "Oh my God, I'm getting a surround sound effect now from the universe." So I went home that night, and I said, "Okay. Universe, I'm listening. Clearly, this is here."

Wow! Talk about law of attraction in practice. How did you design the program?

I asked myself, if I was going to teach someone to do what I do, what would I do? All of a sudden, pen went to paper, and it was like the universe revealed itself. The next day, I had a call with Evelyn, who's now the lead instructor and managing director with the QSCA. At that time, she was my client, and she said, "Oh my God, Christy, I know what I want to do. I want to be a coach, and I want you to certify me." I said, "Well, you know what's funny is that I've been getting this message all week long. I put pen to paper last night, and I'm actually going to do this. I am going to create a certification program." So, I put the marketing together, got the affiliates to promote it, and she was the very first person to sign up for the QSCA in 2008.

That was truly meant to be.

Yeah, and in no way did it ever feel too big. In no way did it ever feel like, "Oh God, who am I to do this?" I mean, I could see the magic of it flowing through me. It just felt right, and it felt like I was enlivened by it. The more that was revealed to me, the more excited I got about the potential. I said, "Okay, I want 50 students. I want 25 in the morning class, 25 in the evening class." And on the day I was closing registration, I got the last person to sign up, and it was 50 students. All of it was so divinely guided that I just felt like I was along for the ride.

That's beautiful. You mentioned you were nervous when you first started, but now you're so conversational and relatable. What advice do you have to help others get to that place?

You just need to be yourself. The way that I share my teaching points is I share my story. It's funny because I'm a Scorpio. There's a part of me that, when I'm going through something, I'm quiet and private about it. Once I'm over it, I've learned it and I've mastered it, I'm like, "Okay, here it is world." I'm a total open book. I share my failures, my wobbles, and what I could have done better or different. I share what I did and didn't do, and especially what I didn't understand.

Tell me more about that.

I'm always teaching from the place of very personal experiences, so I can be who I am. I mean, it actually cracks me up, Maria, because there's people who say, "Oh God, you are so authentic. You're so real." And for me it's like, "Yeah, who else am I supposed to be?" I heard in a recent interview that Oprah was saying she used to want to be like Barbara Walters. One time, she realized that she had made a mistake on a broadcast, and "her", the true Oprah came out in Oprah fashion. She realized, "I make a better Oprah than I'll ever make a Barbara Walters." If you're willing to share your personal stories, and paint a picture for someone when you're teaching them, it brings out your authenticity. It brings out who you are, and that's why people feel I'm so real.

It seems like it's not in your DNA to do it any other way. That's really cool.

Thank you.

What's the worst thing that's happened to you as a speaker?

I tried to deliver the same message to different groups. I remember I had two speaking engagements in one week, and one was to a group of really successful people that wanted to learn how to manifest even greater success for themselves. They were impressed by things I shared. I took that same exact speech, and spoke to a group of administrators of a college. Their department was being eliminated, and they were losing their jobs. So, they were in a very different state than the other group. These people were in fear. So, when I shared some successes, not from a place of "Let me impress you" but, "Let me show you what's possible when you apply universal laws." I think out of a hundred people in the room, I got two people that were inspired. The rest of the evaluations were all negative. They said my talk had no relevance, and that I didn't know any of the problems they were having. It wasn't a fun moment for me. But it was a big eye-opener that whenever you're speaking, you must know who your audience is and their current situation.

What would have done differently had you known?

I would still have come from an authentic place, but I could have come at it with more empathy and compassion, and addressed the elephant in the room. "Hey, I understand, you know, you're having a lot of fear right now. I understand what's going on. And this is how you can make your life different." I should have taught them a different way of creating success by applying the universal laws instead of the way that I came about it with the people that were already achieving the success.

If a speaker is struggling with opening up like that, how can they learn to speak to the problems and pain of the audience?

You have to come from a place that isn't about you. A lot of speakers, especially when they're starting out, think it's about them and their performance. When you take yourself out of the equation, when you come from a place of, "I'm here to serve, I'm here to educate, I'm here to inspire, I'm here to inform," then it's a totally different perspective. It's really easy to say, "Oh, I'm nervous because I'm not gonna do well," or "I'm not gonna know my stuff." We get so caught up in our heads, and that makes it all about us when really, it's not about us at all. It's about the audience. Coming from a place of service changes everything.

Absolutely. Out of all the different elements of your work, writing books, delivering keynotes, doing live events with major players, and creating weekly inspiring videos, where do you feel most at home?

Whenever I'm teaching, the medium really doesn't matter. It's just about how I can show up and teach. For example, in the Quantum Success show that I do, the weekly videos that come out on my website every Monday, I'm inspired to share that information. That's what I love doing. You know, how to deal with negativity, how to attract the dream house, how to lose weight or whatever it is, coming from what I know about universal laws and my own experiences, stories, and perspective. I love to share that. And now, I'm doing more things on Facebook live, where I'm able to share some meditations that help people implement and connect with their divine. Whatever medium that allows people to return to their divine self, then I become a channel for that.

With all those things going on, what have you learned about staying productive and managing it all?

There are a lot of things in business that you need to do, but those aren't the things that I necessarily enjoy doing. For example, I don't want to have to set up my Facebook pages, or do bookkeeping, accounting, and web design. These things are necessary because I have an internet business. Managing the QSCA and uploading the recordings, all that technical stuff, I don't want to do that. I'm very clear on the things I want to do in my business and that I am skilled at and love doing. That's writing, teaching, speaking, and coaching. And I love marketing, too because I can get creative with the information. I love getting the idea, but I certainly don't want to implement the marketing.

What do you do after coming up with the idea?

I want to be able to take that and delegate the implementation of the idea. I have a team that implements it for me. It's important for me to look at my numbers, and I love that. I want to see what the profits are. I want to see how the sales are doing. I want to see what I'm doing versus last year. All that's really important, because I need to know my expenses and where I'm spending my money. But the daily accounting, entering everything in and adding it up, I'd rather pull my eyelashes out. It drains my energy, and takes me away from doing the things that I really want to do. What has really helped is getting clear about what I want to do, what I'm skillful at, and then being very committed to doing just that. Doing that requires farming out and delegating things to my team, and that really allows me to be able to show up and teach. That's made a huge difference in my business, and how I feel about my business.

What do you most love about speaking?

What I love most about speaking is when you have your audience in front of you, which is a much better way for the audience to connect. That's how I started my business. I would go speak at the learning annex and other places. I loved it because it's like there is an instant connection with the audience, and those that really resonated with me would come and speak to me afterwards. They would tell me how it resonated, so there's instant feedback. It's not like doing a teleseminar or webinar online, which I love doing too, but I don't know how each person's feeling. I can't necessarily see their faces. After a talk, I love having people come up to me and tell me, "Oh my God! That really touched me. That really helped me in a way that you just don't even know." I just love that instant feedback.

And the energy feels so different in person. You can actually feel their energy.

Yes. Absolutely.

What would someone do differently if they're starting to do more social media? How is it different?

You're not in front of the person. You know what I mean? So, it is different, but you have to keep your energy up. You have to know what you want to say, and you need to feel the energy because there's still energy, even though it's virtual. For me, I'm less focused on the output and more about moving inward and what I'm going to say. There are not so many people staring at you, you know what I mean, so it's not like you have to worry about, "what are you wearing? What does your hair and makeup look like? What mannerisms are you going to use? Are you going to speak over to this side of the audience and then come over to the other side of the stage?" There's none of that to worry or think about. In a webinar or teleseminar, what's most important is the content and the energy that you bring.

As you built up your business and you've reached higher level of success, how has your life changed?

My life has changed because there are more choices. Obviously, with having more exposure and serving more people, there's been more financial success, and dreams that I've had with my husband have really come true, like living half the time in Arizona and half the time in Montreal. There are just more choices. There's more opportunity to play with successful people. As my vibration is raised, I'm attracting more people that have a higher vibration, and I'm attracting more clients that want my services and more money because of it. It's just been an amazing journey, honestly.

Christy, thank you so much for your time. You're doing such important work, and making the world a better place for so many people.

Thank you so much, Maria.

KEY TAKEAWAYS

- ▸ Be authentic. No one else has your gift or can express it the way you do.
- ▸ Share your personal stories and you'll connect more with your audience.
- ▸ Know the audience you're speaking to in advance and tailor your approach.
- ▸ Focus on your skills and what you love to do, and delegate the rest.
- ▸ It isn't about you. It is about them.

ABOUT CHRISTY WHITMAN

Christy's life-changing message reaches over 200,000 people a month, and her works have been promoted by authors such as Marianne Williamson, Dr. Wayne Dyer, Marci Shimoff, Bryan Tracy, Neil Donald Walsh, Abraham Hicks, and Louise Hay. She currently lives in Montreal with her husband Fredrick and their two boys, Alexander and Maxim.

CONTACT

You can learn more about Christy at her website www.christywhitman.com, where she has a 70-minute abundance webinar available as a free gift. On her website, she has many videos and a weekly video newsletter available. You can also connect with Christy on social media.

CHAPTER 10:
BILL STAINTON

"The audience doesn't care if you make mistakes, they just want to know that you're still driving the bus."
- Bill Stainton

Bill Stainton is a multiple Emmy award-winning TV producer, writer and performer. He is an international keynote speaker, author, business humorist and expert on innovative leadership. Bill blends his business skills from 20 years in corporate management with the showbiz experience he garnered from working with people like Jerry Seinfeld, Ellen DeGeneres and Bill Nye the Science Guy. As the executive producer of Seattle's legendary comedy TV show, *Almost Live!*, Bill led a talented and highly creative team to unparalleled success. A number one rating for 10 straight years and over 100 Emmy awards, 29 of which went to Bill.

Welcome, Bill. Thank you for hanging out with me today.

Thanks Maria, it's a pleasure to be here.

When did you first become a speaker? And what inspired you to move in that direction after all the other great work you had been doing?

My first year speaking was 2006, and I started part-time when I was still on television. When you're on TV, you get asked to speak a lot. Corporate groups, church groups, or school groups. So, I was used to speaking in front of people, but most of them just wanted to hear behind the scenes stories of what it's like to work with Bill Nye the Science Guy, Jerry Seinfeld, Jay Leno and some others. That was fun, but not a professional speaking career. What kicked it into gear was when they canceled the show. They canceled it a month after I had just bought a new car and a new house. Necessity sometimes makes things happen.

What was your first big speaking gig like? What was it like when you stood out on that stage, the lights shining on you?

It felt like home. I had a bit of a head start because I was used to speaking in public from my TV experience. My TV show was shot in front of a live studio audience. I used to do the warm-up for them every week for 15 years. That said, the first time I actually got on a plane to fly to a speaking engagement, to a place where they didn't know about my show, was scary. I had the advantage if they already knew me. But flying someplace else where you can't count on that makes you step up. Fortunately, I was well prepared and got through it. The more you do it the more comfortable you become.

What was it like after that first time when you were nervous and you got through it?

I think you really put your finger on it, Maria, when you talked about finding your voice. For many speakers it takes at least two years to really figure out what your voice is and what your message is on the platform. And that doesn't mean that once you find it it's there forever. Here's what happens. When you first start, you're doing an impression of some of your favorite speakers. You learn what a professional speaker looks and sounds like and you copy them. Eventually, you figure out how to be yourself, and sometimes it happens by accident. You'll tell a story and think, "Oh, this feels different. This feels like me." Eventually you realize you've discovered your own voice.

The more you did find your own voice, did you pick up any difference in the reactions in audience?

Oh, absolutely. It's kind of amazing. When you discover your authentic self, it really comes across to the audience. It resonates and the audience can sense it. We've all been in audiences where it sounded fake or rehearsed or phony. But when you are your authentic self, there's an energy that comes across the stage. Once you find that, you can lose it every now and then but you have to just remember, this is what it feels like, this is what it sounds like, this is who I really am.

Why do you think it's so hard for people to get there?

It can be intimidating trying to go out there and be yourself at first, because you are being a little vulnerable. When you're being yourself and it doesn't go well, it's easy to take that personally. "Oh my goodness, I was being myself and they didn't like it, so I must not be very good." But, if you're trying to act like someone else and they don't like it, at least you're protected behind that veneer. But it's a veneer. You won't grow as a speaker until you learn how to break through that veneer, put yourself out there and be vulnerable.

Getting that message right is so important. Before you learn how to speak or stand on stage, you need to know what you're all about. What is your life story? What is that thing that you hold back and don't say to people, but it's what you most need to let out?

That's beautiful. It goes to what you said initially about getting over nerves. I'm not sure the nerves ever go away. There are some engagements where I feel completely comfortable and then there are others where I'm inexplicably nervous. It has nothing to do with the size of the audience. I just figure if you have nerves, that's just another word for energy and you need energy. You said at the beginning of this conversation that one of the keys is to realize it's not about you, it's about the message that you want to get across to them. If you're up there worried if they're liking you, you're going to have a hard road.

We all want human connection, yet so many of us fear rejection.

Yes. Here's what I learned from my years in show business. I think it might have been Jerry Seinfeld that taught it to me. He said, in virtually every audience there's some grumpy guy in the corner who's just not going to like you. Maybe before he came to the event his wife told him she wanted a divorce. Maybe you just remind him of his seventh-grade shop teacher who he hated. You never know but if you spend the whole time on stage trying to get that one guy to love you, he's not going to love you. Let it go. Work with all the other people there who you *can* influence. If you spend all your time focusing on that one person, you're doing a disservice to the people for whom your message really is resonating.

You mentioned you are a Beatles expert. How did you fall into that and do you ever speak about it?

I do speak about it. Whether or not you liked them, you can't argue with their success. They are still the gold standard for success in their business. Who would not like to be known as the Beatles of their industry? Ever since my mom woke me up out of a sound sleep to watch them on the Ed Sullivan show, it has been a lifelong passion. Since then I can't count the number of times I've been to England and Liverpool. I've met many people who were in the Beatles inner circle, including two of the Beatles who I got to spend time with. I've been a musician all my life so it's a real passion of mine.

How would you relate their success to speaking?

Growing into your own voice as a speaker is just what the Beatles did as musicians. The idea is to take all the different influences and make them your unique voice on stage. Just like the Beatles were influenced by blues, Motown, pop and all the things that came before. But, they incorporated all of those influences into their music in a way that is definably, absolutely, definitely, the Beatles. It's the same with the speaking business, at least that's my experience.

Being an expert in the TV/film industry, what does someone need to keep in mind when switching from live to virtual speaking?

Here's the big difference Maria, and it's really a mindset thing. When you're on stage it's one to many. You're speaking to a few dozen, a few hundred or a few thousand people. If you're in front of a camera, whether that camera is in a TV studio, on your laptop, or on your iPhone, it's one to one. Here's my advice. Make it seem like you are talking to one person. But, figure out who that person or avatar is first. Then when you're on camera just imagine that you're having a conversation with that person. Maybe it's your mom, your best friend, or a character you've invented. It doesn't matter who it is, as long as that person embodies and exemplifies your perfect target audience for that message. Don't think, "I'm talking to a camera" or "I'm talking to thousands or millions of people." No, you're talking to one person, and then it becomes a conversation.

What is your advice to people who are afraid of making a mistake or looking nervous?

Here's the bottom line. If you're getting paid a healthy five figures to speak in front of a thousand people, yeah you better be good. They expect it, they require it. But when you're doing Facebook Live or a video, the audience doesn't really care if you stumble. Here's what I've learned from years of being on camera in front of hundreds of thousands to millions of people. The audience will forgive anything except being made to feel uncomfortable. If you're doing something on camera, you can say, "Okay, let's stop the tape, let's do that again." If it's actually going out to people, just be yourself. If you fumble then you fumble. If you forget your lines, just make a joke about it. Just say, "Oh you know what, I completely forgot what I was going to say. Let's take a look here. Ah yes, that's where I am, fine." The audience doesn't care. As long as they know they're going to get what they came for, it doesn't have to be letter perfect. In fact, letter perfect is really kind of boring.

We all can make a mistake, but that can help us connect to the audience even more.

There's a story I tell professional speakers, it's a true story. There was an actor named Richard Harris. Younger people know him as the first Dumbledore in the Harry Potter movies. Older people might know him playing King Arthur in Camelot, in the movie and on stage. He played it on stage hundreds, maybe thousands of times. He was doing a final tour of Camelot in London's West End, which is Broadway, that's as big as it gets, London's West End. You couldn't get tickets for months, it was like Hamilton. It was in the middle of the run. Packed house of course, and it comes time for one of his big songs. I don't know which one it was, but the orchestra is building to this swell and he steps forward, he opens his mouth and he goes blank. He goes blank. He's on the biggest stage in the theater world in front of a packed audience who's expecting a legend and he forgets his lines. That's the speaker's nightmare, right? But, what does Richard Harris do? Does he panic? Does he start sweating? Does he start stammering? No. Richard Harris walks right to the front of the stage, looks down at the orchestra and says, "Stop stop stop playing. Stop playing." The orchestra careens to a halt because they don't know what he's going to do. He looks right at the audience and says, "I'm so sorry, this is terribly embarrassing but I seem to have completely forgotten the words to this song. Does anybody out there know them?" The entire audience leapt to their feet, gave him a huge standing ovation and then staying on their feet they sang the song with him. My question to you is, do you think anybody in that audience went home and told their friends, "Oh my goodness, you will not believe the unprofessional show I saw today. The guy completely forgot his lines." No, they went home and said, "We saw something special."

Why do you think that was?

Because Richard Harris owned the space. He owned the mistake. Yes, he screwed up, he forgot his lines but boy, he recovered beautifully. He owned it. He said, "I'm sorry. I forgot my lines." That's what speakers need to keep in mind. Whether they're on stage in front of thousands of people or if they're in front of a camera. The audience doesn't care if you make mistakes, they just want to know that you're still driving the bus, that you're still in charge. They don't have to worry if you're going to have a meltdown. As long as you're cool with it, your audience is going to be cool with it, too. It does endear you to them. Just as you said, you think that audience didn't feel closer to Richard Harris from that point on? Yeah, perfection can be boring.

Let me turn this around and ask you. If you think back to all the times you were on camera or giving a talk, is there any incident or time that comes to mind as... a 'Richard Harris moment' where you've made a mistake?

Yeah, although the ending wasn't as successful. I think every speaker has at least one nightmare story. Mine came fairly early in my professional career. It was probably around 2006, and I had taken a gig that I shouldn't have taken. There were red flags but I was assured, no this is fine. It turns out I was absolutely not what this audience wanted. I ended up being on late at night, which is terrible. It was a group of about 260 law partners in a big law firm, and they'd had an open bar. I could tell the instant I was introduced, I could see on their faces, "Oh no, a speaker." It almost didn't matter what I did, it just was not going to work, and it didn't.

So, what did you do?

I was fairly new at professional speaking so I didn't really know how to recover. I would do some things differently now, including not taking that gig. There are few things more cut throat than being the wrong speaker in front of the wrong audience. They did not want a speaker, they would have preferred (in this order): one, a stripper; two, a comedian; or three, going back to the open bar. It was a really uncomfortable lesson, but I learned to never take the wrong gig just for the money. If you're not the right person for that audience then you're taking the job for the wrong reasons.

How does somebody learn about the audience to make sure that match is there?

This was through a speaker's bureau so I didn't have a chance to get information about them in advance. Fortunately, we are still great friends and they book me quite a bit. You want to talk to the person who is planning the meeting or the person who owns the meeting, and those aren't necessarily the same person. You want to make sure that your message is what they want. Ask them questions like, "What's keeping these attendees up at night? What do they want to hear? What's your goal?" Sometimes in my case they say, "Well, we just want to get the meeting started off with a laugh. We want them to feel energized and glad that they're there. We also want them to hear that as leaders they are accountable to their teams." Okay, good. That's actually one of my messages. If they say, we really want to hear about customer service, I'm not their guy. There are better people.

What would you say to speakers starting out taking any job they can?

It's easy early on in your career to take everything that comes your way and there is value to that. The more you speak the quicker you discover your voice and your message, and you get better. The old adage in the speaking business is, 'The more you speak the more you speak'. People see you and you get referrals and spinoff business. It's also important to try speaking outside your comfort zone, but there's a difference between outside your comfort zone and being the absolute wrong speaker for the gig. Sometimes you don't know where that line is until you cross it.

What would you say is your sweet spot, your wheelhouse?

It's leadership and creative thinking. Those are my two things because for 15 years doing my TV show, I led an incredibly creative team so I learned about being creative and leading a creative team. I've got strong expertise in those areas and there's a lot I can do within those areas. If someone gets outside that umbrella, I tell them to look for another speaker. It happens at least two or three times every single year. Somebody will call, they've seen me or heard of me, and they want me for their convention. As I'm talking to them I realize I'm not the right fit and I'll say, "You know what? Let me give you the names of three other people who will be a better fit for you." I would much rather do that than be the wrong person in front of the wrong audience.

How important is it to get a standing ovation?

In the beginning the greatest thing that can happen is a standing ovation. Yes, it's a nice ego boost but that's all it is. It doesn't necessarily reflect how good you are. You talk to almost any professional speaker, and they've all gotten standing ovations for work they would consider B minus. "That audience just felt like standing. That audience was just easily amused. They were in a great mood, they just stood." There are other times we do a great job and the audience politely applauds. The thing is, if you're focused on that for your reward, you're leaving it completely up to them. What you really should be focused on, and you really nailed this in the beginning Maria, is what you want to get across to them. When you focus on the message and whether they're getting it, then the focus is them.

Okay. You're focused on your audience, but how do you read them along the way?

Even though you're the only one speaking, it's a dialogue. You can tell where they're at because you're getting feedback from them. Are they getting it? Are they nodding? Are they with me? Just stay focused on them, you guys getting this? Does it make sense? When that's your focus, you're going to be a much more effective speaker, and you're going to connect with the audience more. It also goes a long way towards getting rid of nerves because now your energy is focused outward rather than inward.

It's good to have some nerves because it keeps you light on your feet.

Yes, as long as you're in control. We don't want to use the audience as a therapist. If you're going to talk about something traumatic, you need to be ready to say it on stage. Otherwise you start crying and losing control. Now the audience is feeling really uncomfortable because they feel like they have to take care of you emotionally. That's not their job. You can talk about anything on stage depending on the audience and why you're there. And if you're nervous, think of those nerves as energy and use techniques that you learn over the years to help mitigate those nerves. You are in control of the energy. The energy can't be in control of you. That's a big difference.

I call that 'owning the room'.

Oh, I love that phrase.

You connect with the energy of the audience and keep them in a safe place so that you don't cross that line. Take them up to that edge of the emotion but not too far so that they can come back.

I've seen that with certain speakers. As soon as they take the stage, they own the space. That doesn't mean they own it in a boastful, egotistical way. It's confidence. It's confidence in knowing that you've got a good message, you've got a good delivery, you deserve to be there. You've done this hundreds of times. In the beginning of your career, obviously you haven't done it hundreds of times, but you have to start somewhere. Richard Harris, the first time he ever auditioned for a role, he probably couldn't have pulled off what he did during that last run of Camelot. That came from years of experience and owning the room. That's a great phrase, Maria.

What do you think most speakers miss?

I think the biggest miss is their 'why'. The audience might not care why you're a speaker but *you* have to know and I think a lot speakers miss this. It took me several years to find out, why do I do what I do? Ultimately, I realized I want to change the world by creating better leaders. I think when somebody's a great leader, their team members become better leaders, and they become better mothers and fathers. They become more community-focused. It's not just a bottom line thing. It makes a difference in the world and I want to be a part of that. It took me years to figure that out.

How does someone figure out their 'why'?

I think speakers who are just starting out should take a half-day and sit down with a piece of paper and a pencil. Not their computer because physically writing something down connects it to the brain. Ask yourself, why do I want to do what I'm doing? Then just close your eyes and see what comes up for you. Write down ideas as they come to you. Keep playing with it and refining it over time. Sometimes it's tough when you're starting out because you may not know your message. Try on a few different things as you speak and then, you know what happens? One day it comes to you and you say to yourself, this is who I am, what my message is, and what I want to talk about.

Once someone starts to have more success with speaking, what do they need to keep in mind?

Most speakers don't treat speaking as a business. This is a business. You've got to learn how to invoice, how to write contracts, how to manage a schedule, make plane reservations, and write pre-program questionnaires. You need to have the systems in place and make customer follow-up a priority. The most successful speakers I know do not think of themselves as speakers, they think of themselves as the President and CEO of a speaking business. Get the business part right or you may just find that you are making a lot of money but not making any profit.

What do you recommend for people who may get stuck along the way?

Reach out and ask for help. I'm very involved with the National Speakers Association and it is a remarkably helpful community. I know that if I have a question about anything, everyone in that association is just a phone call or email away. The nice thing about the speaking business is if one of my competitors/friends gets the gig this year, they're very likely to recommend me for next year and vice versa. There really is plenty of work to go around.

Bill, if you could be remembered for one thing, what would it be?

That is a deep one. One thing. I would like to think that I made a difference with my TV show. To this day, I have people coming up to me almost on a daily basis and saying, "I grew up watching you, you made such a difference. You made me laugh." I've had people tell me the story about the last time they saw their mother laugh was watching my show. They get to remember their loved one laughing. That's a high calling. You start to think, I actually did make a difference. As speakers we have an amazing opportunity. We get to influence lives and we get paid to do it. Some in ways we'll never know. One of the greatest things an epitaph could say is, "He or she made a positive difference."

Bill, this has just been a pleasure, and so much fun. Thank you for taking the time to join me.

Thanks, you too, Maria.

KEY TAKEAWAYS

- It takes time to discover and grow into your own voice.
- When speaking on camera just imagine you're having a conversation with one specific person.
- Never take the wrong gig just for the money.
- You're not just a speaker, you're the CEO of a speaking business.
- Find out your 'why'.

ABOUT BILL STAINTON

Bill owned his own corporate training company, and created many training programs around workplace dynamics and team motivation. He's been quoted in the Wall Street Journal and Forbes and is a regular columnist for Seattle Business magazine. From Maine to Malaysia, Bill is committed to helping leaders and their teams achieve their highest potential while maintaining a sense of fun along the way.

CONTACT

You can connect with Bill through his website at www.BillStainton.com, where he has a robust blog, as well as many video program clips and quick tips. You can also get access to Bill's free gift, the *Instant Innovation Cheat Sheet! 20 Questions to ask when you need an innovative idea NOW!* Bill is available on social media.

CHAPTER 11:
KRISTEN BROWN

"You really want to deliver an experience, and to do that you need to let go of the fear."
-Kristen Brown

Kristen Brown is an engaging international keynote speaker and author who motivates audiences to strive for maximum impact in their work and personal lives. She spent 15 years in sales and marketing leadership roles working with big brands before starting her own award-winning company. She has worked with many Fortune 500 teams and start-ups across industries to drive sales, leadership, and high performance. Recently named a top 20 trailblazer in the industry by *Meetings Today Magazine*, Kristen has been featured in the national media sharing insights from her bestselling books and research including *Live with Kelly*, Forbes, CNN, *Working Mother, Psychology Today*, and many more.

Welcome, and thanks for joining me today, Kristen.

Hi Maria. Thanks for having me.

Walk us through your story and how you got into speaking.

I'm from a small town and started speaking and entertaining in 5th grade after joining the speech team and drama. I've actually always thought speaking was pretty fun.

I think we often set ourselves up for failure because we try to bridge a gap that's too huge. Whatever situation we're in, we may have a big vision. But we think that vision needs to happen quickly or easily. We have in our minds this gap that we need to close. And it's so huge that it actually sets us up for failure. For example, if you are an emerging speaker and you want to become a $5,000, $10,000, or $20,000 speaker at a large conference. That's a really big gap to close quickly and easily. So, if feel stuck, start really small. Say, "Okay, what is something that I can do right now to be just a little bit better?" Just a teeny bit better. Maybe that's going to your LinkedIn profile and updating your tagline. Maybe it's reaching out to a speaker coach. Maybe it's watching some demo videos of speakers that are a step or two ahead of you. But, *not* trying to be the keynote at a major international conference. That's too big of a gap.

Pick something small and then feel motivated because you've accomplished your goal.

Yes.

What was your first speaking gig like? How did that go?

My first gig that I had booked on my own was a small women's expo near my hometown. I was doing a breakout session to ten people. I was going to be talking about my first book, "The Best Worst Thing." It was a memoir about losing my husband and how I ended up starting my business. I went into this breakout, and most of them I knew, my mom, my grandma and some of my high school friends, and I cried almost the whole time. They wanted me to tell my personal story, and it was the first time I'd ever done it. It was terrible. Luckily, it was only ten people.

That must have been tough.

Afterwards, I thought, "Oh my gosh, I just totally wasted their time. I sucked." And then the two women in the room that I didn't know came up to me one at a time. The first one said, "Oh my God, that was so amazing. That was exactly what I needed to hear." And I'm like, "What? You needed to hear me blubbering for 45 minutes?" But I had touched something in her that she needed to hear. The second woman walked up to me and immediately crumbled. She started crying and said, "I've been struggling with losing my father. Hearing you talk and seeing that you've picked yourself back up, I feel like I can go do this, too."

Wow.

That was the first speaking that I had done unrelated to my paid corporate job. I thought, okay, I can do this. I need to refine some things so I'm not crying the whole time, but I can do it.

You just never know. You thought it sucked and some people completely loved it.

Yeah, it was amazing.

What was a big turning point in your speaking career?

I realized that my message was bigger than just stress. It wasn't what I was passionate about and where I felt I could make the biggest impact. For 15 years, I had been in the corporate world as a VP, with big multi-national companies. I felt like I needed to use some of that and start helping workforces. It broke my heart every day seeing so many people struggling and hating going to work. I wanted to close that gap of, "I hate my job," and make them like it just a little bit more.

How did you learn to sell that in a corporate environment?

It's about positioning and the bottom line. When you're selling yourself to corporate you can't say, " I'm gonna teach them how to meditate and build stress relief and work-life balance." If you want to get big money you have to speak to the teams that are directly impacting the bottom line. That would be sales people. It would be the executive leadership teams. That's where you get the money. They may need stress management, but that's not how you get in the door. You say, "Do you want to sell more stuff? Here's what you gotta do." And stress, or some of the softer skills can be bullet points in that. But that's not the main lead, which is: what's the bottom line impact for the organization?

How would you describe your main lead? Your foundational message, what you are all about.

It's funny, I've gone through a big rebranding in the last year and I'm still trying to nail that down. When people ask me what I do, I say, "I help organizations and individuals increase their bottom line by looking at their presence, their productivity and their profits." I focus on sales teams, leadership teams and corporate teams that wants to perform more effectively. I'm still refining my elevator pitch, but that's what I'm all about. I don't *not* talk about personal stuff in my programs, I just don't lead with it.

You don't decorate the door with it, as they say.

Yes, I like that.

You talked about your rebranding. How is that shifting?

My brand used to be Happy Hour Effect, that's the name of my second book. It's about the positive mindset shift that happens in the transition from work to home. I did tons of research about Happy Hour shortly after my husband died, because I missed happy hour. I couldn't go because I had a baby at home and wasn't feeling very happy. I was missing it, but I knew it wasn't related to alcohol. I knew there was more to it and that led to my research. That brand served me very well, but I started to hit a wall as far as the speaking fees I was able to charge. In corporate, they see that and immediately think that it's soft skills.

They weren't taking it seriously.

Exactly. They didn't see the 15 years of leadership, the awards I've won, the market share I've increased, the bottom line impact I've had. Leading with Happy Hour Effect was no longer serving me. I knew I had to shift. Happy Hour Effect is still there during the transition, but it's no longer my umbrella brand. I'm now "Kristen Brown Presents."

Congratulations on that. That's a big move.

Thanks. It is huge.

You primarily do keynote speaking, but you've built up many other parts to your business. How did you pull that together, and how do you manage your time?

I've very consciously built a platform over time. When my book came out, I made it my mission to get tons of media because it would start getting me visibility and exposure. So, I did a lot of PR. I started small, with a local radio station that probably has 500 listeners. I built up to my local media, and just got bigger and bigger. I appeared on, "Live with Kelly and Michael." I did HLN, and BBC so I've done a lot of big stuff. But I didn't start there. You can't just say, "Oh, I want to be on the Today show." They're not gonna have you on unless they're certain you've honed your message and you can carry a live TV segment in front of three to five million people. I think people try to go too big too soon.

You have this wonderful, relatable, straightforward style, with humor, and you're so approachable. How did you develop and grow into that voice?

That's a good question. It's really been experimental. There are some things I'm terrible at on stage. I tend to share a lot, because I'm fast talker and I want to give them so much when I'm up there. But sometimes you have to step back and just cover what their brain can actually absorb.

When you're speaking, does it change depending on the size of the group?

If you're an opening keynote at an event, you're going to share different content and have a different style than if you're the closing keynote. If you're a breakout, it's a different experience than if you're a keynote. But, whether it's a room of 50 that you're keynoting versus a room of 500 or 1000, you just need to be your authentic, true self and talk to the audience as if you're having a conversation with them. Give them action steps and takeaways. Be engaging. Don't be a talking head. Have some exercises. Go out into the audience. Bring people on stage. Make it about them instead of about how awesome and cool you and your stories are.

Some people are nervous and hesitant to walk into the audience. What advice do you have for that?

You really want to deliver an experience, and to do that you have to let go of fear. I think the more knowledge you have up front about the audience, the better. I have a detailed questionnaire that goes to the meeting planner, beforehand, that asks, "Who are they? What's the demographic? What change are they going through right now? What are they resistant to?" Then I have them share three to five people within the company that I can call and ask about the current state of the state. "What's going on in your team? What are some things you're loving? What are some things that are challenging?" It's all anonymous, I don't share any of the feedback with the meeting planner. Research the company so you know their culture and the changes they're going through. People hear that and say, "Oh my God, that's lot of work." It is a lot of work, but if you want to start making 5, 10, 15 thousand dollars, if you want to get spinoff gigs, if you want to get consulting or coaching from it, you have to be engaged at that level.

I love that approach. You start the conversation with the audience before you even get there.

Yes.

How do you approach storytelling?

If I tell a story, it needs to have a point they can actually take away. Your stories need to have a point that's relevant to the audience. So, if you have a canned story that you tell often, ask yourself, is that story really appropriate for every single group? It's probably not. You need to have many stories to draw from that you can customize for each audience. Don't have just five stories. This limits you to speaking to that company only one time. Because they don't want to bring someone back next year to do the same exact program. You need to have multiple stories.

What would you say are the key elements of telling a good story?

Every story has to have a clear point that ties to that audience. They can be funny, but they don't always have to be 'feel good' stories. It has to touch them in some way. It needs to get them thinking, and it needs to trigger something. Make sure your stories are emotionally charged. That doesn't mean you have to make them cry. And in fact, please don't make them cry. Connect through humor. Connect through "Aha" moments. Make it feel like you are talking to me that whole time.

I know people who feel they've been successful when they can get the audience to cry and then laugh. What is your thought behind saying, "Please don't make them cry?"

It's funny. I often make my audience cry because I tell a funny story about surf camp that ties to my husband dying. So, I'm not saying don't make them cry. Make them cry for the right reason. We all have our personal stories, but the second you make an audience cry or make them feel sorry for you, you've flipped the focus from them to you and you've sucked all the energy out of the room. And you don't want to waste any time or real estate building them back up. People say, "Well, it's about overcoming and resilience and how I got through it." Okay, but you have to be sure that you are truly building them back up with action steps they can take so they don't just think, "Oh, that was Jane. She's the cancer lady." You want them to remember, "Oh my God, Jane made me leave that room and I felt so freaking good. I knew exactly what to do when I left that room. She changed my life for the better."

When you first come on, and you're feeling out the audience and the energy in the room, how does that change your approach?

If you're doing your research first, like I mentioned earlier, and you know the audience before you even walk in the door, you're already gonna have a great sense of what to expect. If you know that you're walking into a room with a company that's going through massive change, they just had a round of layoffs, and you're following the SVP of Sales talking about the state of the union and he's saying, "Yeah, we're down," you know the energy is probably gonna be pretty low. Your job then is to open with a story, experience or interaction that's positive, uplifting, and energizing, as opposed to one that's more serious or intense. Whereas, if they had an amazing year and the SVP's up there saying, "Oh my God, we nailed it. We blew the roof off this place!" The audience is already up. It's hard for an audience to maintain that level so you may want to take them back to a calmer opening, and then bring 'em back up. Because you need that variety.

What if you don't know who's going to be in the room?

In that case, get there early, hang out and observe. Talk to people and see what the energy is in the room. See how they're interacting. Are they talking to each other? Are they sitting at their tables with their phones? Once you're on stage, it's pretty easy to see if people are connected with you. If they're looking at you, if they're leaning forward, if their arms are uncrossed, if they've got their elbows on the tables and they're looking at you and leaning in. Then you've got them. They're engaged, they're listening. They want to be there, they want to listen.

What if they're *not* engaged?

If they're slid back, their arms are crossed and their legs are crossed under the table, if they're on their phones, not smiling or have cranky resting face looks, then you've got to do something to energize them. You either need to get yourself out into that audience and start getting them up and talking to them, or you need to get someone on stage and do something funny. You really have to be adaptable and that goes back to not having a cookie cutter speech. It's being able to read the crowd and adapt on the fly, based on the energy you're getting from them.

Speaking of being adaptable, what is the worst thing that's happened you while speaking, and how did you recover?

I was doing a huge breakout with about 600 people. It was a big leadership conference, so lots of spinoff potential. A half hour before I was to go on stage, I was puking in my hotel room. On the floor of my bathroom, sweating, like, "How am I gonna do this?" It was awful. I was thinking, "Okay, I have to do this. I can't *not* do this." I use a lot of essential oils and I had some with me. I go through peppermint oil like crazy and I seriously think I probably had a fourth of a bottle of it, sucked it down, splashed my face with water, put on some lipstick, put on a little extra eyeliner, got myself down there, and kept it together. I got on stage and my stomach issues went away for that hour because the adrenaline took over. I actually did an okay job. I watched the video and thought, "It wasn't my best, but I didn't suck." So, it wasn't great. But I didn't fail, I didn't *not* do it.

Good for you. So, what shifted after that, for the next time you went on to speak? Did you feel like that again?

Oh yeah, I got freaked out. I thought, is this going to happen again? I feel like I had eaten something that didn't agree with me and it was a legitimate illness, it wasn't nerves. I was spooked and I had the yips, I called it, like when athletes get the yips and start missing free throws and stuff. I was really off my game for a couple of months after that.

What do you do right before you speak to prepare?

I'm an introvert, so I tend to just have some alone time. I do a little bit of meditation, a little deep breathing, have a little peppermint oil, make sure I have water, have a throat drop. I'll do one quick review of my opening in my mind. Because once I get my opening, I'll be able to flow through it. So, it's really just getting my mind in the game. being mindful of what I'm about to do, why I'm doing it, and how to serve that audience and give them amazingness they can walk away with.

Many people begin speaking for free and offer something at the end of their talk. How does someone transition into being paid?

Start speaking to groups that typically don't pay, like Rotary, Chambers of Commerce, churches or schools. And professional associations, like the National Speakers Association, they have many different opportunities. Often, big conferences will pay their keynote speaker but they won't pay breakout speakers. So, you need to do some research and start to get to know the industry. There are opportunities out there if you've got content that's relevant to them. Start with those, because when you're doing them for free, you're learning how to speak. You're learning how to hone your message and interact with an audience. You're learning about yourself and how you behave on stage so you can master that.

Once you build up your skills and network, how do you up the ante?

Once you're feeling pretty good about that and you're getting decent feedback, maybe you're getting some inquiries, like, "Hey, will you come and speak for us?" That's when you start to charge. So, someone sees you at Rotary, they say, "Hey could you come and speak for our company?" Then you start to charge. You don't go from zero to ten thousand. You go from zero to five hundred, to a thousand, to fifteen hundred, and you work your way up. And once you're consistently booking at a certain fee level, raise your fees another five hundred or a thousand dollars.

What are your thoughts around practice and getting feedback?

Any speaker who doesn't think they need to practice and get feedback is never going to be a good speaker. Even speakers I know who are making $20-$30,000 an hour on stage, are practicing and getting feedback. They have coaches and mentors that are helping them continually improve. Join Toastmasters because that's a great place to practice and get feedback.

If you knew then what you know now, what would you have done differently?

I would have started leading with bottom line, impactful stuff sooner and not buried my corporate experience behind some of the fluffier stuff I was leading with. Not everything works for everyone. I'm not saying you should go do everything that I'm suggesting. These are things that have worked for me and others. So you really do need to experiment, and do what feels right for you. Experiment and be open to trying different things. Have fun with it. Don't take it so seriously that it starts to feel like a drag.

Kristen, thank you so much for your time, your openness, and great insights.

Thank you so much for having me, Maria.

KEY TAKEAWAYS

- Start small and don't try to bridge a gap that's too huge.
- Research. The more you know who's in the audience, the better.
- Read the crowd and adapt on the fly.
- Speak for free to hone your skills, then start to charge and gradually raise your fees.
- Have multiple stories.

ABOUT KRISTEN BROWN

Kristen's writing has landed her books on multiple Amazon bestseller lists, on the covers of magazines, on national TV, and in the hands of celebrities. Kristen adds humor to her keynotes by weaving in relevant stories that resonate with, and empower, her audiences. She has a Masters Certificate in Integral Theory that is all about the art and science of multiple perspectives tied to human development. She motivates audiences with low stress, high success ideas for professional and personal growth that directly impact the bottom line by boosting sales, leadership, productivity and profits.

CONTACT

You can learn more about Kristen by visiting her website at www.KristenBrownPresents.com where you'll find links to many videos and podcasts. Kristen can also be found on social media.

CHAPTER 12:
ELEANOR BEATON

"Relentless pursuit plus patience equals blow-away success."
-Eleanor Beaton

 Eleanor Beaton is an international speaker, coach and trainer who's helped hundreds of women become personally, professionally, and financially empowered by teaching them the leadership skills of 7-figure business women. Eleanor's articles and advice have been featured in dozens of media outlets including CTV, CBC, *The Globe and Mail, Atlantic Business Magazine, Chatelaine,* SheOwnsIt.com, and *PROFIT Magazine.* She is the host of Fierce Feminine Leadership, a top ranked podcast for ambitious women, and she's the chair of the visiting women's executive exchange program at the Yale School of Management.

Welcome, Eleanor. It's so great to have you here.

Thank you so much for having me, Maria.

Let's go back to the beginning. How did you get started?

I started a communications consulting firm 12 years ago. We worked with CEOs, politicians, and leaders of non-profit organizations who were lobbying to make changes in public policy. What they all shared was the need to be able to tell a compelling story, and to own the room. They needed people to listen to them, and we were coaching them to do that behind-the-scenes. Then, my clients started asking me to come into their organizations and train their people.

What that similar to what you were already doing?

It was more focused on interpersonal communication. I loved it. I took hundreds of people through communications programs that I designed. That led to leadership communications programs, and that's where I started to see a big need. Around some of those leadership tables I was seeing a huge opportunity for women to be able to really own the room.

What did that look like?

I was seeing opportunities for brilliant women who were fabulous leaders to engage in politics better, to express their ideas with more power, and ultimately, have more influence in the boardroom and in their organizations. For many of the women I was working with, this was the difference-maker for getting promotions and making big deals. I saw the need and decided to launch Fierce Feminine Leadership.

How did speaking help your business grow?

We needed to get our message out there. I think for any entrepreneur, your biggest liability is that people don't know who you are. I'm so glad that you're encouraging people to get out and speak; it's really important to get your message out. For me, speaking was a great way to get out in front of the women that I could serve and inspire them to take action, which sometimes involved doing business with us.

How did you come up with "Fierce Feminine Leadership"?

The name represents what is required. In order to create change, we need to change the paradigm of leadership and this means inviting, inspiring and supporting women to lean in to leadership at all levels.

And how does one do that?

Stepping in to your leadership is an enormously humbling experience. You've got to be able to look yourself in the mirror, accept who you are, and understand that most of the time that you're leading you're in the midst of uncertainty. To do this, you need to really hold the line and be steady. And that requires a certain level of fierceness and self-belief. Certainty is like standing on the top of a mountain. One moment it's clear and you can see for miles and the next moment you're surrounded by clouds. I think it comes and goes just like the weather.

What was it like when you got this clarity in your work? How did your speaking change?

That's a great question. I trusted my material more and had the chutzpah to be able to move into the keynote space. I've heard this said before, the difference between a workshop speaker and a keynote speaker is that a workshop speaker feels that everybody has to go away with six different points in order for her talk to have been worthy. The keynote speaker makes one point six different times. When I speak, my goal is to move people and provide them with a couple of practical takeaways, but to focus more on my audience than on my content.

That's interesting. What would you suggest for people to move into that place?

There's some great research out there about the impact of judgment on performance. In any kind of performance, whether it's athletic, artistic, or speaking, anytime you introduce the element of judgment, the person becomes self-conscious and their performance slips. If while I'm talking, let's say I'm at a podium, I have my phone and you're in the audience and you think I'm doing a great job and you text me, "Hey, you're doing a great job. Your talk is awesome." That takes me out of the talk. It takes me out of the flow of what I'm doing and into your head, and now I'm evaluating myself based on what I think you think.

How do you avoid that?

I have learned to get myself into a state of flow where I am not attached to the outcome of my audience. I speak to a lot of very successful corporate women and if you look out in an audience like that, you're not getting a ton of feedback in terms of people nodding their heads or smiling back at you. I'm more likely to have people who are looking at me very seriously. They've got their corporate armor on. I've gone through so many experiences where I did a talk, and based on the visual feedback I got, I had no idea if people liked it or not, and then I got swamped the moment I stepped off the stage. What that taught me is that you can't be too attached to your audience's reaction in the moment.

Is there anything that you do right before you speak?

It sounds so funny. I visualize myself as the heartbeat of the room. Being connected to everyone in the room and being there to serve and generate an experience in the hearts and minds of people who are listening. I visualize myself being this radiant, Oprah-like person. I don't just own the room. I own the building.

I love that. I work with people on how to own the room, but I think I'm gonna switch that now to own the building.

That's right. Absolutely. There's a great story from Madeline Albright. She talks about when she had just been named as the U.S. Ambassador to the United Nations. It's her first meeting and they're not in the big room. The power meetings happen in the small rooms. She steps into this small room and her strategy is to not speak. She's just gonna go in, and get the lay of the land. She walks in and sees it's not her name on the placard. It says, "United States of America." She realizes that if she doesn't speak, it's like the voice of the United States was silent. That's when she realized that she had to speak.

If you look back throughout the years, what's the worst thing that's happened and how did you recover?

That's a great question.

As speakers, we have to be ready for anything, right?

That's right. I don't remember any bad things happening to me speaking. I've been very fortunate. To this day I get nervous when I go in front of certain crowds. The threshold for how big that crowd has to be just gets a little bigger, but I always have that jolt. I see that as a good thing. It's elevating my energy. It's waking me up and keeping me honest out there on stage. I'm bringing my best every time. I would say that's something I didn't anticipate.

Some nervous energy is good. How do you coach yourself to move through the nervousness in order to be present and serve the audience?

At the end of the day, I have to ask myself, why am I here? What impact am I gonna have on the women in this room? That's always who I'm focused on. It's thinking less about myself and more about them and reminding myself that I've got this. I'm not thinking about moving millions of women, just a few every day.

What kind of mindset do you need to really do this well?

A friend of mine talks about it in terms of showing up like a calm, confident competitor. That's how I try to conduct myself. There are lots of situations I've been in where I feel nervous. Think about if you were a little fish and you got stuck in a tank with a shark. The last thing you want to do is act like shark food. You want to show up like a calm, confident, competitor. I do that with my body.

What do you do with your body?

I stand up straight. I focus on radiating energy out and on being the owner of the building and taking on that hostess energy and that really helps me work through the nerves I may be feeling. Then, when I'm doing it, I focus on being in the moment and not splitting from myself, like starting to observe myself or focusing on what others may think about how I'm doing.

When did that mindset shift start happening for you? Have you always done that or did you cultivate that over time?

I cultivated that over time. When I started my first business, it was very much behind the scenes and I liked that. Then, about six years ago my father died. He was a young guy when he died. He had a very swift battle with cancer and you know what happens when anybody has a brush with mortality with someone that close to you. It makes you think about your life, the impact you want to have, what you're here to do. I was married and had two little kids at the time, and was pretty burnt out.

How did you handle that?

This shift happened inside me where I was like, I am tired of helping other people find their message. I have this message and I want to get out there and do it. In order to do that I had to get over my fear of being seen. The fear of being seen is huge. It came in layers, Maria, for me.

How did you start to peel away the layers?

I started blogging and putting my ideas out there, which made me feel very vulnerable, but I also saw how powerful it was. Then, I started speaking. At first it was in front of very small groups and I felt really comfortable teaching. But then I noticed when I started talking about my stuff, it was more engaging. I have some galvanizing and charged opinions about things. I started throwing those in, and it kept getting reinforced with my audiences that some of my points were landing. It definitely happened in layers.

Slowly letting yourself emerge takes time.

What I always try to pay attention to is that feeling of shame. This is what happens. When you put yourself out there, you will feel ashamed. That's how it goes. It's not just embarrassment. It's like, whoa, I was just really out there.

And, who am I to do this?

Yes, who am I do to this? Actors feel it all the time. This is why actors often can't watch themselves because you feel ashamed when you see yourself laid bare like that. I learned that when I felt that way, that was actually a good sign. It didn't mean that I was doing something wrong. It meant that I was putting myself out there in a bigger way. It became a muscle that I just kept building up.

That is a great way to look at it. Related to building that muscle, what difference have coaches, mentors and training made for you?

It's absolutely huge. My mentors and coaches have really helped me develop my plans, improve my skills, and execute. Then, you find yourself a sponsor, somebody who is well connected, who is influential and willing to make introductions to stick his or her neck out on your behalf. That's what can really make a quick difference.

So many try, but people can't do this on their own.

Look, if you want to do this, you've got to have coaching and mentoring. When people are trying to do this on their own, I sometimes shake my head. You wouldn't open up a bakery without investing in an oven. You're not gonna open up a thought leader business without investing in mentorship and coaching to help you get out of your own way and make it happen. And, if you really want to take things up quickly, focus on building your network with sponsors.

You've got a wonderful reach to your audience through speaking, coaching, live events, a blog and podcasts. What did it take to put all of these pieces together?

It takes a combination of relentless commitment and patience. Here's what I hear all the time, "Oh, I did a few Facebook Lives and they didn't work," or "Oh, I podcasted for three months and it really didn't work." At that point I say, well, try it for a year and then come back to me. If you're in the speaking or thought leader space, and you're building out your brand as a recognized expert, you have to understand that you are a media company that monetizes through courses or coaching or group programs. We have generated huge amounts of content. We do podcasts three times a week. We do a weekly blog. We do weekly LinkedIn posts. We do probably two free training webinars a month. We have done that for a good solid three years straight. You've got to be committed to being a media company and to generating content.

Why does it take so long to get results?

In the beginning, the content that you're creating is only going to help you convert sales. Meaning, let's say that I want to take my speaking to the next level this year and I decide I'm going to hire a coach. I hear about him somewhere. Now, I'm going to his website. I'm gonna check out his content and that's going to give me the backup I need to hire him. If he's only been creating content for about a year, chances are I'm not gonna be able to find it. He hasn't been out there enough to attract leads into his business with his content. So, you need to understand that you will not generate inbound leads probably for two to three years. It takes that amount of critical mass to really make the tables turn. At that point if you still want to play, game on sister. Game on brother. Let's go. If you are not prepared to commit to that, this journey is gonna be a lot tougher for you.

If I'm a speaker and want to get out there and speak, where is a good place to start?

I would choose a hero platform. Choose one platform where you're going to show up not speaking. It could be a blog, videos, a newsletter, a podcast, or something else. You've got to figure out which platform is perfect for you and commit to generating original content there on a weekly or bi-weekly basis. If somebody comes to me as a guest on my podcast, and that's a great place for speakers to get started, I'm gonna check them out to see what they have to say.

What are your thoughts around speaking for free?

Don't be afraid to speak for free in the beginning. And to be clear, I never speak for free even if I speak for free. Meaning, if I'm speaking for free, I build my talk around a call-to-action that will help build my business. For instance, I might be doing a talk and then I would say, if you would like to have these slides, please text this word to this number. That helps me capture the names and emails of interested people in the audience so we can then follow-up with them. Understand that keynote speakers, their primary job is to sell tickets. Until you have that ability to draw, you may find you're speaking for free and monetizing it in other juicy and interesting ways off the backend.

What would you recommend for others who want to find speaking gigs? How do they interact with the meeting planner?

A couple of things. First you want to have your one-pager for your talk. And, understand that this talk will not be a one hit wonder. The purpose is to build your business. You want to be clear with the event planner about who the audience is to make sure it's a good fit for you and that it's worthy of your time. Every time you are in X place, it means you're away from Y place doing Zed.

What are some of the technical pieces to think about?

Do you want to have a lapel mic? Do you want to have a handheld? Do you want to be at a podium? Knowing your preferences around that is critical. When it comes to landing speaking gigs, networking is how I do everything. I tell people what I do and every time I get a speaking gig, I ask for referrals afterward. If you can do that, you will be able to build out your career with as many speaking gigs as you want to maintain your business at the level you desire. Over time, of course, right? Over time.

You mentioned the call-to-action. What have you learned around keeping the audience engaged along the way so that works?

When I started my business I didn't have much in the way of sales skills. My father was a professor, and my speaking style is a little bit professorial, so I would talk about ideas and concepts. In the past, I lacked the courage to really make an emotional connection with people. Some of you reading this may be like me and my tribe: type A, highly educated, and comfortable with ideas and concepts. If so, notice if you get into professor mode and step over opportunities to engage with the audience. If they don't know that you care and if they don't feel connected to you, they're gonna walk away and say, "Ah, Eleanor's talk. That was so intellectually interesting," and they'll probably never think about it again. Have the courage to make an emotional connection and provide a strong call to action, so you can connect over the long-term.

What does this look like for different audiences?

My audience is smart and skeptical so I've got to make the connection in order to earn the right to ask them to do something. I don't want to intimidate people in the beginning, so I always try to first convey how much I genuinely care about them. When you do that, it creates a bond between you and your audience. Doing that, while being upfront about my business and the connection I want to form with them, has been useful and helps me convert really well. I always come up with something that displays that level of emotional honesty.

How do you do that?

It could be with a story. I have a couple of signature stories that I
use throughout different talks. I string them together like beads
on a necklace. After speaking for a while, you begin to have a
command of your material because you know what your
signature stories are. You know the meaning they have and how
you want to use them to help the audience connect with a point
that you're making. And it comes through practice being in front
of a room, seeing the reaction and measuring the results. To start
out, I would take it lightly. I would take the approach of the
scientist where you're testing. You put something out there, you
test, you rework. You learn through making mistakes more than
being perfect right away.

**As you've become more successful, how has your life changed
and what has surprised you along the way?**

In some ways, nothing has changed. I am relentlessly focused on
where I want to go, so most of the time I'm just focused on what's
next. I know the yoga gurus would say that's not healthy, that we
should be present and in the moment and I get that, but I'm not
buying it. I love the pursuit. What has changed is who I've
become in framing my ideas in a way that has impact. I have a
message that is affecting people's lives.

How has your message changed you personally?

Things don't bother me the way that they did. I don't hold back
the way that I did. I am comfortable here saying the yoga people
might not think that's cool, but I'm cool with it. It's taking
ownership of who you are. That has been the biggest change. In
terms of growing the business, studies have shown that after
about $75,000 in income, increased money doesn't make you
happier. We think it does, but it doesn't. Yes, my business has
grown and that's kind of cool, but my happiness has come much
more from the personal change I've experienced.

**That is awesome. If you could go back, what would you have
done differently?**

I would be more patient. I made a swift transition from the old business to the new business because I didn't realize how long it would take. I would have stayed relentlessly committed to taking action in the right direction, but I would have made a softer transition between the two, had I known that everything takes time. If you're a creative, entrepreneurial type, things generally take longer than you think.

I'm sure that fits most of us. We're so excited to get to that next level, sometimes it's just stepping back and being where we are.

Yeah, and just having patience. It's like relentless pursuit plus patience equals blow-away success.

I love it. Eleanor, thank you so much for sharing your time, your story, and your expertise.

Thank you, Maria.

KEY TAKEAWAYS

- Your biggest liability is that people don't know who you are.
- Be committed to being a media company and to generating content.
- Focus more on your audience than your content.
- Get in a state of flow where you're not attached to the outcome of your audience.
- Have the courage to make an emotional connection and provide a strong call to action.

ABOUT ELEANOR BEATON

Personally trained by best-selling author and Oprah Winfrey Life Coach Dr. Martha Beck, Eleanor offers women at all career stages a powerful mix of personal coaching, career mentorship and specialized training and consulting. She has worked one-on-one with highly successful leaders such as Dragon's Den star Arlene

Dickinson. Through corporate workshops, private coaching and small group training programs, Eleanor has taught hundreds of women the strategies behind some of the country's most compelling women leaders. She has spoken and trained around the world.

CONTACT

You can learn more on Eleanor's website at www.EleanorBeaton.com, where you can take the 5-minute Fierce Feminine Leadership Assessment. She also has a top-ranked podcast called, *Fierce Feminine Leadership: The Success Podcast for Ambitious Women in Business*. You can check it out on iTunes or Stitcher. Eleanor's available on social media.

CHAPTER 13:
DEIRDRE VAN NEST

"Lord, let me remember my words, forget myself, and bless my audience."
-Deirdre Van Nest

 Deirdre Van Nest is an international speaker and trainer and the creator of the Speak and Get Results™ Blueprint, a system that teaches financial advisors, coaches, and thought leaders how to be "Crazy Good" speakers so they can better the world, bring in business, and build their brands using speaking. She is a Certified World Class Speaking™ Coach, a Certified Fearless Living Coach, a contributing author of the Amazon bestseller *World Class Speaking™ in Action*, and author of *"Fire Your Fear™."*

Welcome Deirdre. I'm so glad you're here!

Thank you so much. I'm excited to be here.

Why did you want to become a speaker? How did you get started out?

I didn't want to become a speaker, Maria. I bet you didn't expect that answer, did you?

No, but I want to hear more!

I had a very challenging experience in 9th grade. I had been into acting since 4th grade, and gotten some great roles. So, I went into high-school excited and ready to dive into theater. I was cast in 8th grade as Scrooge, and I was feeling confident. Then my acting teacher, responding to a scene, essentially said, "You stink." I was very vulnerable at the time, since my mom had died in a car accident when I was ten. I didn't have *any* kind of skin, much less thick skin. I just accepted what was said as truth. I literally left the stage and didn't act again. In fact, I wouldn't speak in public for 24 years.

Wow. Thanks for sharing that.

In 2008, when I started my practice, I was certified as a Fearless Living Coach. I was working with business owners, helping them move past the fears that were holding them back. Well, the one consistent advice I repeatedly got was, "Get out there and speak. That's how you're going to get clients, visibility, credibility." I said "Oh, no. Not doing that." But God had other plans. I was teaching people how to, "fire their fear" but I knew this was a fear I needed to conquer. I had to walk the talk. So, although I was a very reluctant speaker, I said, "All right, I'm going to do this thing" and jumped in.

I'm sure a lot of people resonate with that. What shifted for you that allowed you to get that point?

Two things. One, going back to walking the talk. You cannot call yourself a Certified Fearless Living Coach without taking the risks you're asking your clients to take. The second was, I got to a point in my life where the thought of failing at my business and not making an impact on the world was more terrifying than the thought of speaking.

Getting out and sharing your message is how we change the world. That's what's so exciting about speaking.

Yes! I'll never forget the first invitation I got from a woman who was running a big breakfast networking meeting. I started my business in the recession, when a lot of people were losing their jobs, so there were tons of job transition groups and meetings. A woman named Katherine called me one day and said, "Hey, would you be our speaker in September for our kickoff meeting?" There was silence. I didn't say a word. She probably thought I had hung up the phone. I was thinking, "Oh my gosh, what do I say?" Finally, I said, "You know what Katherine, let me get back to you, I need to check my schedule." She said, "Great." It took me a week to get back to her. Of course, I was not checking my schedule. I was checking my courage. Although it took me a week to say yes, that was the start of what has been one of the greatest journeys and joys of my life.

What was it like when you finally got out there? And what was it like right afterwards?

I was very nervous. It was very scary, but I'll tell you what I did, and I recommend everybody does the same thing. Get a coach. I wasn't hiring a speaking coach at that time, but I found a book, and the book was my mentor. Craig Valentine's book called, *World Class Speaking*. I think it's one of the best books written to date.

Yes. I love that one, too.

It's one of the best books on constructing a presentation. I used the formula in the book to write my talk, and that gave me a lot of courage. I wasn't just slapping something together. I put some research and thought behind it. Even though I was terrified, people really liked it. I made great connections, and from there got other speaking engagements. So, it was a very reinforcing opportunity to move forward.

What's the worst thing that ever happened to you as a speaker, besides the one when you were 14?

I have a pretty close second that happened recently. I've been speaking since around 2008-2009, and I haven't had any horrendous things happen, until last September. It was a

Wednesday morning, and every other week on Wednesday morning I go to Bible Study in yoga pants, and a sweatshirt, and if I've not showered, a baseball hat. But, for some reason, and I believe this is a God thing, I showered, did my hair, and had a little bit of makeup on. So, I'm working on this gig that's tomorrow by going through the slides one more time. I get a phone call and it was my client saying, "Are you almost here?"

Oh no!

Oh yes, Maria. It's even painful for me to relay this story right now, because I still get the feeling that I felt then. It was "What? Oh, my gosh! Isn't it tomorrow?" "No, it's today." Maria, I just about died.

That's a rough one.

The level of horror going on inside of me, I can't even explain it. Now, thank God it was in my hometown of Minneapolis and would only take 20 minutes to get there. The good and the bad news about the situation is that this was my biggest corporate client. On the one hand, they know my track record, they know that this is not me. On the other hand, it's my biggest corporate client! I said, "Is there anything you can do before me? Can you switch the agenda?" "Yes. We can hold them off until 2:30." I said, "Great. I will be there." I ran upstairs, threw on a dress and some lipstick. But can you imagine if I hadn't done everything before? I would have shown up in a baseball hat.

How did you manage getting through that?

Now, here's the learning, okay? What I needed to do in the moment was to switch my mindset from, horrified and wanting to crawl into a fetal position, to focusing on being in top condition and showing up as if nothing has happened. I didn't want that audience to even guess that there was a problem.

I'm sure people have had similar experiences, and they're probably wondering, "How do you shift your mindset?"

It's a conscious choice. My job as a speaker is to give the best performance for my client. That's my job. The damage is done already, I can't fix that. Now I need to show up fully present and ready to go. You can't do that if you're beating yourself up the whole way. So, I'm driving down there, and praying the whole way about it. I often use prayer and scripture to put me in that positive mindset. I keep repeating positive things, I put on great music that uplifts me, and I keep saying, "This is going to be the best talk I ever gave," It was a full-blown campaign of positivity in that car ride.

A campaign, that's great.

Right? It was a campaign of positivity in that car ride. Fortunately, I got there in time, delivered the presentation, and it went great. Afterwards, I apologized to my host. They were beautiful people, and we prayed together, which is incredible. The company has hired me again multiple times.

So, it had a happy ending.

It had a very happy ending, but I will tell you, it threw my confidence in myself from mid-September until after Thanksgiving of this year. I couldn't even talk about it for a couple of weeks, because I felt ashamed, and it was too raw. But it has been a great learning experience. In a way, I'm glad that it happened, because I learned from it, and I can share it with others.

What are some things you do before going on stage? is there anything you do either physically or mentally?

Yes. While I'm waiting to be introduced, I really look out to the audience. This might sound corny, but I look at them with love. I try to look at each person and think, "Okay, you're a fellow human being, I love you." I also have what I call my EPP, and that's my Energy Protection Plan. I believe very strongly as a speaker that you have an obligation to your audience to protect your energy before you're going to be speaking. Too many people say, "Oh, I've got this speaking gig," and then they rush from one thing to the next right up to the speech. But you can't perform at your best if there's no margin, and you don't have a plan to protect your energy.

Is it like putting a bubble around yourself?

Everyone needs to figure out what that's going to be for them. I'm going to tell you what I do, and this has been successful for me and my clients. The biggest piece of EPP is getting yourself off any type of media for a minimum of one hour before your presentation. This includes social media, emails, texts, and phone calls.

That's negativity you don't want in your mind.

Exactly. In fact, Maria, as I was waiting to call you, I saw an email come in from someone I was waiting to hear from about a proposal. I was so tempted to open that email. But I said, "Nope. Because, if he doesn't tell me it's going to go the way I'm hoping it goes, that's going to affect me, even if I'm thinking it doesn't. Does that make sense?

Absolutely.

The other thing I do is pray and say scripture verses. I have a mantra that I say, "Lord, let me remember my words, forget myself, and bless my audience. For me, it's uplifting praise music, remembering that God's in charge, not me, and he wants to bless me and the audience. During my prep time, the more I can take the focus off me, the better. The other thing I just started doing recently is blessing other people before I speak. For example, I had a speaking gig and it was snowing. So, I left early and had breakfast at the hotel. I had the most delightful waitress, Natalie. I told her how great she was, and then the bill came, and it was $11.53. Well then, I felt God say to me, "Give her a hundred bucks." And I thought, "Oh, that's so cool!" So, I gave her a $100 tip! She came back to me and said, "Did you mean to do that?" I said, "Yes, I did. You were fantastic, thank you. Keep up the good work." That's the energy that I got to take with me for my two-hour training. How cool is that?

When you send it out into the universe, that energy comes back to you.

Exactly. And this is just a tip around business development, because for most of us it's not fun, right? Looking and asking for leads, and trying to get gigs. The way I've made that fun is to look for someone I can bless first, and only then do I make *my* ask of somebody else. It has actually made asking fun.

And it doesn't have to be financial.

No. In fact sometimes it's better if it's not. Sending a nice email or doing other things are just as meaningful. Allow yourself to be creative. Maybe it's writing a handwritten note with a Starbucks card to someone. Those are some of my practices.

Once you've done your prep work and you walk out, how do you connect and open with a bang?

There are many ways to open with a bang. People can be very creative here, so I encourage everyone to have fun with it. I have two "go-to's" that I use. One is opening with a powerful question that's related to the topic. It gets the audience nodding their heads in agreement, and it also gets them thinking about themselves. They're immediately engaged because they want to answer the question. That's one option. The second is just diving right into a story. A lot of times I'll ask a question, and *then* dive into the story. So, you can do that, too.

What's the technique or framework *you* use to tell a great story?

There are different types of stories for different types of scenarios. There are stories designed to showcase your expertise and do the selling for you, without it sounding like you're selling. There are other stories you tell to illustrate a point. There are even smaller stories, called client vignettes.

What tips could you share with us around these?

One thing, which is one of my pet peeves, is that a lot of people are out there telling stories that have no point. This is critical, the story must be relevant to the content. I don't need to hear your sad story if it has no relevance to the content. It will feel like an overshare, "too much information" to the audience. It is critical that you pick a story that is not only relatable but will move them and the content forward in some way. That's one of the biggest mistakes I see speakers making.

How do you pick a story?

With my clients, I teach that there are two ways to come out there. You can have this story that you believe is worthy of sharing, and then you build a platform and content around that. The other way to do it is to look at your content and ask, "What stories in my life can I use to illustrate this content?" And then you shape that story so the message aligns with your content.

I throw things in I've experienced with my kids. What I tend to use is basketball, because I've watched my son play basketball for so many years, and I've seen thousands of games.

Yes. It's fantastic. Like you, I have "my son playing hockey at six years old" story. That is a story I've been using for years, and it's a core piece of one of my keynotes. So, yes, take things from your life and put them in there. The acting story I told you in the beginning is one of the main stories that I tell.

Speaking of acting, a lot of people do everything right, but they're still holding back. There isn't a true connection, because they haven't really opened up, or let themselves be vulnerable.

Not only do I know what you're talking about, I lived it. I've been doing this for close to a decade and I get paid well to teach other business owners how to do this. What may be surprising, and it's surprising to me, is that I did not fully break through that barrier until January 11th of 2017, this year.

Wow, what happened?

I felt like when I was speaking, I was leaving a part of myself outside the room. It had been happening for several years. And for the life of me, I could not figure out what that meant. The fact that I was doing so well made it a little harder, because I didn't need to figure that out to survive. I also had these external indicators saying, "Oh, no. You're doing great! You're fine." But this voice inside of me was saying, "No. You're leaving part of yourself outside the room." It has been a journey of very pointed and deep personal growth to figure it out. And in January of this year, the pieces finally came together. I figured out why I was feeling that way and which parts were leaving the room. Once I figured it out, I invited all of me in.

What did that feel like when you were speaking? And how did your speaking change?

Oh, my gosh, the difference has been so freeing for me emotionally and personally. It's a huge gift. But the difference it made to the audience was unbelievable. My speaking moved to a level it has never reached before. I don't think I'm alone in that phenomenon happening. You can be doing this for a long time and reach a nice level of success, and still be protecting yourself. I want to encourage anyone reading, if you're newer and you're doing that, you're in good company. This is part of the journey. People say, "Owning your own business and entrepreneurship is the greatest personal growth journey you'll ever go on." And I wholeheartedly agree.

Absolutely.

All of this is part of a journey. Don't quit, don't get down on yourself, don't beat yourself up if you're feeling like I did, because I felt that way for years. Just keep at it. Keep asking the questions. Keep digging in. I had to process and recover from some very early trauma in my life, around the time of my mom dying, to be able to fully bring myself in the room.

Don't judge yourself. You're exactly where you need to be, right where you are.

Yeah. You're where you need to be.

Well, I'm really excited for you. That sounds like such a huge breakthrough.

It's a huge breakthrough, and what's really amazing about it is just last week, on Wednesday and Thursday, I got two contracts for opportunities I have been praying for, and persisting on, for seven years. They came in one after the other. I believe it is directly related to the breakthrough on January 11th. I believe God is saying, "You weren't ready before. Now you're ready to step into this level of big. Now you're ready. "

You opened up to this whole new level and had room for it to show up.

Exactly. I guess my lesson is, yes, you want to get technical coaching. I don't believe anyone can be a four or five figure speaker, or know how to really sell from the stage, without being coached. It's a science, so yes, get coaching. Study your craft and practice. But along the way, pay close attention to the person you're becoming, and who you want to become.

Thinking back, if you knew then what you know now, what would you have done differently?

Let me think. Okay, this relates to the recent breakthrough I've had, so I don't know if I could have done it differently, but here goes, okay? One of the things I'm a big, big, believer in is not winging presentations, but practicing. Practice, practice, practice. But what I have realized, since I had my breakthrough, is that I tend to over practice, and that came from not feeling like all of myself was in the room. Does that make sense?

Yes. Trying to get it just right, trying to get all the right pieces in there.

Perfect, get it perfect, exactly. And I don't want people to hear, "Don't practice," because that needs to happen. That's part of your job. But don't sacrifice connection and authenticity for perfection. Don't worry about having the perfect performance. If over-practicing is going to yield that level of anxiety, then pull back a little bit.

It's all about being 'good enough', right?

Yes, it is. I did a keynote on Wednesday morning, a talk I've done since 2008. I know this talk, Maria. I've delivered it hundreds of times, but before I had my breakthrough, I still probably would have practiced it for five hours. You know what I did? I'm so proud of myself. That week, I looked at it to refresh myself, practiced it once, and said, "I'm good." That was it. I didn't obsess going over it a million times, and it was fantastic.

Because it was already in you, in your heart.

Exactly. It's in my heart. It's in every cell of my being, right?

Beautiful. Deirdre, it's been such a pleasure, and you've given some great tips that will help people, so I appreciate that.

Awesome. Good, I'm happy to share it. Thank you.

KEY TAKEAWAYS

‣ Protect your energy by taking a time-out from media, emails, and texts before your speech.

‣ Shift your mindset with a campaign of positivity.

‣ Open with a powerful question or dive right into a story.

‣ Don't sacrifice connection and authenticity for perfection.

‣ Don't beat yourself up. Keep at it. Keep asking questions.

ABOUT DEIRDRE VAN NEST

An entrepreneur since 1999, Deirdre owns a real estate investment company, and speaks internationally. In 2008 she started her practice and became a Fearless Living Coach. Deirdre is an Italian/Irish New Yorker and lives in Minneapolis, MN.

CONTACT

You can connect with Deirdre by visiting her website at www.crazygoodtalks.com, or her LinkedIn profile at www.linkedin.com/in/dvannest. On Deirdre's website, you have access to helpful videos and a Free Quiz, which will help you determine if you have a regular talk or a crazy good money-making talk. Deirdre's also available on social media.

CHAPTER 14:
KIT WELCHLIN

"There are always two different audiences; the one that hired you and the people in the seats."
-Kit Welchlin

Kit Welchlin grew up on a hog and dairy farm in Southern Minnesota and began public speaking at the age of nine in a 4-H public speaking contest. Today, Kit is a successful keynote speaker and an instructor for the Minnesota State Colleges and Universities. He has delivered more than 3,000 speeches and seminars to over 500,000 people over the past 26 years. Kit is a professional member of the National Speakers Association and, in 2014, he was inducted into the Minnesota Speakers Association Hall of Fame.

Thank you so much for joining me today, Kit.

Thank you, Maria. I look forward to our conversation.

First, congratulations on being inducted into the Hall of Fame.

Thank you. That took me by surprise. I thought a person might have to be retired before getting inducted into the Hall of Fame. I think I have about another ten years in the speaking business, so it's quite an honor.

Tell us about nine-year-old Kit in his 4-H public speaking contest. What was that like?

My first speech was on photography. I had six pictures that I had printed from my 110 Instamatic camera. When I was going through the pictures and pointing out the principles of good photography, I noticed that the last photograph had my shadow in it. When I saw that, I finished my presentation by saying, "Now, here's a common mistake that amateur photographers make, which is to sometimes have their shadow in the picture," and everybody nodded their head, like, "Oh, yeah, I've seen that." And here it was a mistake I had made! I had looked at those pictures a dozen times when I was gluing them to the construction paper, and I never noticed that shadow until I was presenting. So, I just went with describing the problem in the picture, and no one ever knew it was a mistake.

Great recovery. You had tremendous business success starting in your early 20's. How did you move into professional speaking after leading manufacturing companies?

Ever since I started at age nine, I was drawn to public speaking. When I was a freshman in college, I took a lot of speech classes, because I was speaking at banquets and leadership academies and camps for 4H and the FFA, Future Farmers of America. When we were involved in manufacturing in the '80s, I used to take my employees to Dale Carnegie, SkillPath and Career Track seminars, and we always learned things we could apply. When I left manufacturing, I always remembered the impact from those seminars and workshops. It was a very natural step for me to take.

Did you do a lot of presenting as the leader and CEO?

Yes, we had weekly meetings, and I also was active in the community. I used to drive about 20 miles out of town to attend some of the Toastmasters meetings. You need to practice regularly, just like if you were a pilot and had your own small plane. You probably want to fly that plane once a week just to make sure you don't forget how.

You often use the stories and experience of growing up on a farm to make your point. What would you say is the key to great storytelling?

I don't tell a story in a presentation unless it's relevant to the topic. I have hundreds of stories and I only use them in certain speeches. The best thing to do is to tell the stories that actually happened to you because you can relive them while you're telling them. It draws everybody else into the story with you. All of us have struggles as we go through life, so I always balance my stories between business and personal, because people attending may be struggling in either area.

I love the one when you're talking about change and relating that to riding a horse.

Yes. Just like adapting to change, it's a lot easier to ride a horse in the direction it's headed. When I tell that story, I can just picture myself on this pony that belonged to the Wolle girls. They lived near our farm. There was just a bit and bridle on that horse and it had decided to go home, and I was on it at the time! I remember riding that horse nonstop for a mile and a half back to their house, and there was no way for me to stop it. Now that's a figure of speech people may have heard before, but when you've actually been on the horse, it's a lot easier to tell the story.

You seem so comfortable when you speak. How did you get to that place?

I was taking a speech class in my master's degree program and it has stayed with me to this day. We talked about the five canons of rhetoric, and the book *The Rhetoric* by Aristotle. They were Invention, Disposition, Style, Delivery, and Memory. The one that always stayed with me was Memory. Aristotle believed you should design your presentation so it's easy for you to remember and easy for your audience to remember, too. As I recall from that course, it was recommended that you have five times more information prepared than you're going to be able to share. Then you will have this reservoir of knowledge to fall back on so you can be completely comfortable–even if you don't recall what you want to say at the moment, you have a whole bunch of other stuff you could say that's just as valuable. I've always kept that in mind.

How do you prepare for your talks?

I over-prepare. When I'm creating a presentation, I work eight hours for every hour that I'm going to present. I have a routine to make sure that I'm in the right frame of mind. First, I fully prepare my content and how I'm going to deliver it. I review the order of the stories and the flow of the concepts. I double check my PowerPoint. I arrive at least an hour before the presentation to check the setup and AV, and I'm ready to go. I take the preparation seriously, but we have a lot of fun during my presentations. It should be fun, because then people accidentally learn quite a bit. And that's a great way to spend an hour or two.

Once you begin, how do you get connected and focused on the audience?

I always ask my clients to give me as much information as possible in advance, like what are the situations, conversations or problems they address day in day out? The audience ends up wondering if I've ever worked in their organization because it sounds like I must have been just down the hall the last couple of years. When I start presenting I feel like I disappear in a way and my whole focus is just trying to get that information across to that audience as clearly and concisely as possible. The focus isn't on me. It's completely on the audience.

You do the work to prepare and then you just let it flow.

That's right. It's like pulling a plug on a bathtub, out it comes. It's also important to remember that there are a couple of different audiences. There's the person that hires you, but also the people that are in the seats. You need to keep in mind that the person who hired you took a tremendous risk by bringing you in, so you want to do everything you can to make them look good. Their professional reputation is on the line. I also think about that person in the seats who needs the information to keep their job, be happy and balanced in their life. I always keep those two different audiences in mind.

What have you learned about working with these events and meeting planners?

Over the last 15 years, I've learned the most important thing is to be as responsive as possible, to connect with that meeting planner quickly either by phone or email to let them know whether you're available or not so they don't have to wait. Make sure you're very clear on the objectives of the meeting, the challenges in their industry, and what you can provide to help them overcome those obstacles. So, being genuinely concerned, responding with a sense of urgency, and then being clear and concise in your communication to avoid problems down the line.

What are some ways to build these relationships and help make them look good?

I think the greatest compliment to the meeting planner or the person that hired me is when their co-workers or staff say, "Oh, that was great. Thanks for setting that up." It's when their own people compliment them for what a great job they did on their selection or the event itself. I always say, in the speaking business, I'm really just a tick on a dog. If I'm not available that day, they're going to hire a different speaker. Out of the 130 presentations I deliver a year, there's only a handful of people that ask me, "When are you available?" and they schedule around me. Otherwise, the other 125 hire me depending on whether I'm available to work around their calendar. It's important to remember that we are as replaceable as any other employee.

What would you say makes you unique as a speaker? What's your secret sauce?

Whenever I'm hired to speak on a topic, my goal is to provide them all the information they need so they never need to hire me again on that topic. I never build a presentation hoping for spinoff business. I'm going to give them everything they need that day, and if they don't hire me again it's because they got everything they needed. That's why I ended up with so many different topics. I never intended it to be that way, but when a client and their employees trust me, they invite me to present on other topics that they're struggling with, which is quite a compliment.

How do you gather the information and expertise on these different topics when requested?

When I started back in 1991, I used the five topics from my master's thesis, and it grew from there. One of the first big conferences I spoke at the client asked me to fill in for someone the next day. After that she booked me and my five topics again for the next year. After speaking the next year, she said, "What else do you speak on?" I said, "Nothing," and she said, "Well, here's a list of topics that our administrators would like for training. Would you please pick out five for next year and create them, polish them and then come back?" That happened for three years and I created three- to four-hour seminars on all those topics. The nice thing is, there is some common theme that runs through all the topics because I wrote them from my perspective. So, my clients hire me repeatedly over the years on different topics because it's somewhat congruent.

I imagine after talking on those topics so many times that you start to become an expert in them.

Yes. You also learn what you are not qualified to talk about any longer because you haven't maintained the research or stayed current on the trends. The good news is I like reading and I only speak on things I'm interested in, that are critical to my business success, so I benefit personally and professionally, too.

I've heard you say, "If the audience can get comfortable with you, they can get comfortable with the content." Tell me more about that.

I think we've all been in a situation where we've taken a class from a teacher who we really didn't like, where 50 minutes in the classroom feels like 50 hours. When I create a climate in the room where people feel comfortable with me, they are more willing to consider communication strategies that are unfamiliar to them. They have confidence that I won't lead them astray. I also try to think how I can invite my audience to be funny. There's always 5% to 10% of an audience that are really funny people, and if I am willing to turn over some of the control, and create more of a conversation, they say the funniest things. Then I'm with them instead of being an outsider. My logo says, "Learn, laugh, grow." If I have good content and I deliver it in a low stress, low risk way and they have fun, I believe they'll apply it when they get back to work.

Much of what you're talking about sounds like building trust with the audience. When you first begin, how do you break through and build trust?

I think humor that's self-deprecating makes an audience comfortable. I remember years ago coming across some information about mirroring, where you match the emotional or social tone that is in the room. Doing this allows you to blend in at the beginning and then you can move them to a different emotional state. You first need to go where they are, and then after that it doesn't take much time to get someone to give you a little laugh, and so the communication climate shifts pretty quickly.

Go out there and sense where they're at, meet them there and then take them where you want to go.

You say it better than I do.

What's the worst thing that happened to you as a speaker and how did you recover?

There were three times I didn't make it to the event. Once, I was stuck in the Newark Airport and my flight was delayed on the tarmac and I couldn't get off the plane. Finally, when I was coming out of the airport I got a call from the client who said, "We're running about a half hour early...how far away are you?" I was still an hour away and missed the event. I think all three of them were weather related, so I donated my time to make up for the loss because I know how it throws off the meeting planner and the timing. I came back at another time for free. As the speaker, we've got the easiest part of it. I still feel bad about those three times because I know that so much planning goes into those events.

How do you manage 130 speaking gigs per year?

First, I never take a speaking engagement today if there is only one flight that can get there for that event. So, we plan it for next year instead.

You must have some serious frequent flyer miles.

I use those to go to the National Speakers Association meetings, the annual conference, the winter workshop, and other special emphasis groups. So, I burn up my frequent flyer miles for professional development.

Who do you admire as a speaker?

I always admired Brian Tracy. His content is solid, straightforward, and easy to apply. Dr. Alan Zimmerman, my mentor, was a college professor in the speech communication department, and I was on the college speech team. When I decided I wanted to go into the speaking business, Alan was the very first person I called. He said, "Read this book. Read that book. Do this for two years. Do that for two years, and everything from then on will be referral and repeat business." I just trusted his advice, and I've been speaking ever since.

Do you remember what books he told you to read?

One was, *How to Make a Fortune from Public Speaking,* by Robert Anthony. The other book was by Mike Frank, who was one of the first presidents of the National Speakers Association. If I remember the point of the book correctly, it was, If You're Not Making a $1,000 Per Speech Or Seminar, You Need to Read This Book.

What a great book. After all this time, looking back at everything, how have you changed over time as a speaker?

I build in more time in advance of my presentation. I get to the event earlier, the day before if I can. This way I can get a better feel for the audience, the industry and the trade show or expo. In the old days, I always felt like I had to be the show, the one to deliver the content and make it fun. Now, I find that I'm much more willing to share that and be more open to a conversational approach to the presentation instead of it being so one sided.

That's awesome. If someone is just getting out there, how would you suggest they start getting speaking gigs?

This is what Dr. Alan Zimmerman had me do. He says, "The first thing you have to find out is if anybody's interested in what you have to say." He recommended that I enter descriptions in community education catalogs around the metro area to see if anybody would sign up and if people were willing to spend their money to come a seminar at the high school and listen to you go on for three hours. I got great feedback from the people who attended. With my master's degree, I did the same thing through community and technical colleges. I did that for the next two years, and I got lots of practice giving public presentations with quite a diverse audience. I've just continued to fill the calendar ever since.

What would you say about moving from speaking for free to speaking for fee? How does someone move from the free Rotary Club into paid speaking?

You move once you have the nerve to get paid. I remember the anxiety I would have around getting paid to speak. There was no pressure, no stress if I was doing it for free, but, when someone was going to pay me money, I always had in the back of my head, "I have to make sure this was worth it." Over time, clients would guide me on what my fee could be. I always believed that until I was making a certain fee 60% to 80% of the time, I would not raise my fee. Once I had clearly established myself in a certain fee structure, then I would move to the next level. I still have a fear that I could always price myself into a market that does not exist for my topics or my style and I would go out of business.

It's very interesting. I have one last question. If you could have dinner with anyone in the world, either living or not living, who would you pick?

That is a tough question. I think the reason it's so difficult for me is because, if they wrote a book, I've probably read it, so I would have studied their information.

You wouldn't have lunch with Aristotle because you read the book?

No. Actually, now that I think about it, it would be Brian Tracy. I think I would really enjoy talking with him. I never have. I think that'd be a real treat. Maybe at one of the National Speakers Association meetings I'll ask him if I can take him to lunch.

There you go. It's been such a pleasure talking with you, Kit. Lots of helpful insights and techniques for people, so thank you.

It's been delightful. Thank you, Maria.

KEY TAKEAWAYS:

- Don't tell a story unless it's relevant to the topic.

- Relive stories as you're telling them.

- Have five times more information available than you're able to share.

- Gather as much information as possible in advance.

- Learn, laugh, grow.

ABOUT KIT WELCHLIN

At age 21, Kit purchased his first manufacturing company, and by age 26, served as CEO and chairman of the board of three manufacturing companies in three states. In 1991, Kit began speaking professionally as well as teaching at universities. He's taught for 26 years for the Minnesota State Colleges and Universities where he has received the Teaching Excellence Award and been repeatedly nominated as outstanding faculty. Kit has a Master of Arts degree in Speech Communication and wrote the unique business book, The Communication Kit. He has been featured on many radio and television programs and is a highly sought-after keynote speaker.

CONTACT

You can learn about Kit at his website, www.Welchlin.com, where he has his video blog and program content. You can also get a free chapter to Kit's book, The Communication Kit. His second website, www.SeminarsOnStress.com is focused on stress, time and procrastination management and how to manage stressful situations and difficult conversations. You can also connect to Kit on social media.

CHAPTER 15:
LIANA CHAOULI

"Dear God, allow me to open my mouth and for your words to come out."
-Liana Chaouli

 Liana Chaouli, also referred to as "The Style Sage," is the Founder and President of Image Therapists International, Inc. and a globally recognized thought leader, bestselling author, style expert and educator. She provides transformation through the empowerment of wardrobe. Liana has spent decades consulting CEOs, celebrities, and political figures on self-image. Liana is the "go-to" expert for many news sources as an image and personal stylist and appears on major TV and radio shows.

Welcome, and thank you so much for being here, Liana.

I'm so delighted to be here with you.

Let's start back at the beginning. When did you start speaking? What's your story?

It's just so funny, nobody has ever asked me that. The truth is that I would gather up my family and I would hold these long monologues. I would wait for my dad to come home so I could tell him all about my day. You know like most children, they gather up their family and have them sit down and say, "We're going to perform for you." For me it was telling stories. I'm Persian. I come from a long line of storytellers, so telling stories was a natural thing.

What led you to starting your company?

My idea for starting Image Therapist International was to create a space where women could learn what looks best on them and how to show up in the world as authentically as possible. After experiencing the difficulties women had with their bodies and dressing, I felt it was about much more.

It sounds like you were inspired.

I wanted to share their stories and challenges, witnessing what had been going on in the world of fashion, realizing that there was no support for women. I believed that transformation was possible for any human being in any given moment. Sharing this message as a speaker was just the next natural thing, so it started organically. We'd be in a group of people and they would say, "Wow that's really fascinating. What do you do?" I would just talk about it. It wasn't like, "I have to go and be a speaker." After a while, I started to understand that as speakers we have a huge responsibility. That was a very interesting twist in that world, knowing the impact we can have on the people who listen to us.

Tell me more about that.

I started to realize that the information that I was sharing, especially the things that I talk about which are so intimate, were having a huge impact on people's lives and needed to be delivered with care. That's why I believe that a speaker has a great responsibility, whether it's to a crowd of 20 or 200 or 5000. Once I spoke at the Canadian Bridal Fantasy and I told 5000 brides that they shouldn't be wearing white to their wedding. Can you believe that? We need to know what it is that we're saying, why we are teaching it, and what the fundamentals are that we're teaching. It's possible that we can open up a whole new world for someone.

You have such a wonderful connection to people. How do you get people so comfortable and intimate?

That's a good question, Maria. I believe that desire has a lot to do with it. If, as a human being, I have the desire to connect, it's felt by others. It's interesting that you're asking me about being a speaker, because I'm also a singer. As a singer, one of the key principles in order to connect with the audience is that you have to be yourself. Don't put on a mask. Don't put on airs. Just be yourself because all the audience wants to see is you. They don't care about how great your voice is. They care about seeing the authenticity of who you are. That really serves me as a speaker. Isn't that fascinating?

It's very interesting, yeah.

The highest currency we have as speakers is authenticity. The next highest currency, which we squander a lot, is what we pay attention to. As a speaker on stage, the thing that I pay the most attention to is not what I'm saying, but the crowd. I really bond with whoever is in the room. Whether it's 50 or 5000 people.

When you first come out, how do you do that? Do you sense the energy? Do you look at each individual?

All of the above. Some people say, "Liana, how can you do that when you're only in the room for half an hour?" You can. We're human beings. We're spiritual beings living in a physical body. Most of us forget that our spirit is so much greater than the body. We just don't pay enough attention to it.

What does that look like? What do you see most people doing?

We come from our heads, we think too much. "This is what I'm going to be saying. This is my outline, this is the structure of my talk." No! Walk into a room and be present to who's there. Maria, lots of people have a very hard time with this and they say, "Liana, you went off your outline." I say, "You're right, but I had to." When you're present to what's in the room, your outline can go out the window. Otherwise, it's my agenda, and I'm not there for me. I'm there to be in service and to support whoever is in the room.

What would you say to people who are having trouble getting to that authentic place and relaxing into that energy? How do they get to that place?

First, stop thinking. Most people think that speaking and communication is an act of just the mind and the brain. It's not. 95% of communication is nonverbal. It's in the body. I think all of us want to convey something, but the mind gets in the way. That's my premise. If you're having difficulty getting to that which I consider your soul, your being, your essence, or your source, quieting the mind is the best way to get to it.

What do you do before you speak? Do you have a ritual or way to prepare?

I have a couple of things that I do. Connecting to the divine is something that really supports me. There's a prayer that I say before I go out into a conversation, onto a stage, or into a meeting. I said it before you and I had this conversation, and that prayer is always the same. "Dear God, allow me to open my mouth and for your words to come out." It's always the same prayer.

Nice.

I consider myself a vessel and Maria, many times when I've had conversations, I'm training or speaking, it's being recorded. When I go back to the editing bay, for the life of me I cannot remember saying what I said.

Wow.

Yeah. That's the piece where I believe that we as speakers are God's mouthpiece. Especially in the transformational leadership world, which is a big part of my life. For me, speaking and sharing the path to transformation is my ministry. There again, I go back to the same piece at the beginning when I said we have a responsibility.

It sounds like it is about getting in touch with that sense of service.

Yes. But, most speakers think that their commitment is to their work and their speaking, which is a tiny little puzzle piece in their life. My life is made up of these big puzzle pieces and my commitment is an orb that surrounds them. They are all inside of the bigger commitment, which is showing up with integrity and grace.

Tell me more about that small puzzle piece of speaking.

We don't go up to people enough and speak to them. I mention this here because you're not just a speaker on a stage. I consider myself a speaker, a mentor, a teacher, a trainer, and a friend, no matter where I go. Don't just compartmentalize your life into these separate pieces.

What do people need to be aware of if they are on stage in front of 5000 people versus a smaller intimate room?

I think that one of the biggest compliments I ever got was, "You know, Liana you're the same on a big stage as you are when you come to my house for dinner." I think the key is unquestionably being you, just be you. You don't have to become gregarious because you're on the stage of 5000. You just have to be you.

And trusting.

Yes. Trusting that who you are is exactly what that crowd needs. We think, "I have to adjust now because there are 50 people in the room." I'm naturally loud and big, so I used to think, "Oh my

God, I have to dial it down when I'm in front of 10 people."
Maria, you saw me. I don't dial it down. The people who are shy
and soft and tender are being told by other people or by their
speaking coaches, "You're going to get up on that stage and
project, and you better be bigger. You better get louder." I say, no,
you don't have to get louder. You just have to get more authentic.
That is how you connect.

That's interesting.

You don't connect by getting louder. I believe that there are
moments where you have to modulate your voice, of course. You
have to get a little louder, then you have to get softer. Then you
have to stop. Then you have to take a breath. Those are technical
things. What I'm saying is if your essence comes out, your true
essence, then those people that are in the room that need to hear
what you have to say will hear you. The ones who won't, won't,
and thank God for that. I don't want to be all things to all people.

**And some people have big energy, and a gregarious approach
and that's okay, too, if that's your authentic self.**

Right. That's where this piece of authenticity comes in. I have so
many clients who are speakers and I dress them. I take them
through this year-long program. It's about accessing the truth
about why you've been hiding. Sometimes shyness is just a way
to hide. Image therapy is this process of unveiling, uncovering
the soul to discover what's underneath.

**I know that you dress several celebrities. Are there any
common experiences that come up as you're helping them
come across a certain way? Have you noticed certain trends?**

Yes. That most big celebrities are introverts.

That is interesting.

Most movie stars are much more comfortable doing one-on-one
work with me. I've had many conversations with legendary

performers. The conversations were so beautiful, delicate, deeply intimate, and they were always one-on-one. You look at other people who are on big stages, like Tony Robbins. Tony is a very gregarious guy. He loves the attention. He loves the lights and the glamour. Most talented actors whose craft is to portray another character don't live a life built on lights shining in their face and being the center of attention. They take their craft extremely seriously and embody the essence of the part they are playing.

Who has inspired you as a speaker?

My father inspired me as a speaker. My father was an artist and I remember when I was a child, he was a handsome, gregarious, intelligent, and creative man. Very charming and he had this magnetism. I remember hiding under a chair and waiting for my father to enter a room. We'd have a lot of parties at our house and I remember when I was looking up from where I was hiding, I wouldn't look at my dad, but I would look at the crowd. I wanted to see their faces light up when my father walked in. That was one of the funnest activities I remember doing when I was a child.

That is so cool. What did you learn from him as a speaker? What did you take from that?

I'll tell you what I said to myself. I said, "I want that when I grow up. I want to touch people's hearts like that." Remember 95% of communication is nonverbal, so I was watching these people's faces just light up. Whatever he was doing or being or not saying, was just so magnificent and mesmerizing that I said to myself, "I want that." My dad was the first one to inspire me and he was an amazing storyteller to boot. So is my beautiful mom.

What a great story. I love that.

It's so true, Maria. My dad passed away at 54 which is such a waste. Often when I walk on the stage and I see people smile, I think that he's there with me. I always remember the thought I had as a child, "Dear God, whatever it is that he's got, I want it."

It sounds like you have a lot of it, too.

I wouldn't be the one to say. But, thank you.

Who were the people outside your family that you admire?

The people who I really admire as speakers are Gandhi, Lincoln, Maya Angelou, Oprah, and Sophia Loren.

Really? Interesting. What do they all have in common?

I think they're all real. It's like you look at Oprah and you go, "Well, there's Oprah. That's who she is."

Yes, exactly.

In German, there's a fantastic saying that translates as, she doesn't put a leaf in front of her mouth, which means she doesn't stop talking when it's inappropriate. She just says it. Ellen DeGeneres is another one. I love these people who are so real. Be you. Everybody else is taken.

What is the worst thing that's happened to you as a speaker and how did you recover?

I think the worst thing that ever happened to me was when I was speaking in front of about 1000 people. There was a handout I was giving them that was already under their chair. I don't know how this happened, but the questions in the handout were not the questions that I had created. They were very intimate and inappropriate.

Oh no!

Yes. It was bad. One of the reasons why this was so interesting and why there was such a big breakdown is because I'm dyslexic. I take this handout and I look at it. I thought that my brain was playing tricks on me. I saw words like orgasm and sperm. I saw all those things on the page.

Oops…wrong talk.

I'm looking at it and thinking, they don't know that this is under their chair. This is what's going on in my head. There's about 1000 people and they don't know what this is. It's upside down. I fixed it by just nixing the whole activity. Instead, I got them to do an exercise that required them to close their eyes, take the piece of paper that was under their chair, fold it up and tear it into 1000 little pieces. I turned it into an exercise. When it was happening, it was not funny because I had committed to the person who hired me, and the next slide on my deck was the slide that had those words on it. I couldn't even continue my PowerPoint.

Nice recovery. I find that the audience usually doesn't know what's going wrong. They just need to believe that you feel confident and able to handle whatever comes your way.

Yeah. There are so many examples. I mean 35 years of speaking and training. There have been some very interesting ones that were worse. People who are hecklers, who always think that they can bring you down, somehow expose you. Another worst and best experience was someone who basically wanted to battle with me in the audience. But, within about seven minutes, this person was in tears and deeply grateful. That was a really big one.

How did you turn that around?

You know how children have temper tantrums. They always go there just looking for attention. They want to be heard. All of humanity just wants to be heard. We just want to be seen and we want to be heard. There are always trolls and hecklers, people who are just in the audience to make sure that they prove you wrong or shame you. As a speaker, you can look at them as someone who needs a prayer, or someone who needs a hug, or someone who needs love and attention. Then my attitude towards them shifts and there's no more Velcro for them to stick to. Does that make sense?

Yes. Just shifting into a place of compassion.

That's right. Not that I always do this, but I try to live my life that way. When someone is coming at me, I take a lesson from the practice of aikido. Aikido is a martial art that uses your opponent's force and turns it into something you can defend yourself with or move the danger away. Now, I can either turn that heckling into a beautiful dance or I can turn it into a head-on collision. I choose.

Very powerful.

I choose to always turn it into a beautiful dance.

You have a robust business with several streams of income. The advice for speakers is often to expand yourself into other areas. How does a speaker go about building that out over time?

I think that each speaker has to do what feels right to them. There are people who don't want to do anything online and I was one of them for many years. For me, if I was going to teach somebody something, I wanted to do it in person. Each person can find what works for them. Go online, find the spaces where you want to teach, and where you want to learn. One of the things I've learned is to look 'up the ladder'. I always want to be around people and invest in myself in a way that was up the ladder. Not the level I'm at, but out of my comfort zone so I can grow. That's what a lot of people avoid because it's scary.

If you could have dinner with anyone living or not living, who would that be?

Cleopatra.

Really? Why her?

Because she was a very intelligent, feminine, powerful leader. I think in this day and age we need more of that. She used to seduce a man at 20 paces without ever revealing an inch of flesh.

I think that is pretty cool. I was not expecting that.

You thought you would catch me off-guard. Now I caught you off guard.

Love it when that happens.

I think that Cleopatra represents an archetype that is very needed in the world today. The way the world is working, we could use some strong women. There's not enough of them leading our countries, our tribes, and our social networks. I'd love to have her on my board.

Thank you for sharing all of these great insights. I know that people will appreciate what you've shared today.

You're very welcome, my dear. It's my pleasure. Thank you for inviting me.

KEY TAKEAWAYS:

- As speakers, we have a huge responsibility.
- Don't get louder. Just get more authentic.
- Turn heckling into a beautiful dance.
- Be you. Everybody else is taken.
- Be willing to adjust based on the audience's needs.

ABOUT LIANA CHAOULI

At the Academy of Image Therapy in Beverly Hills, Liana has built a unique curriculum to educate and accredit future Image Therapists. She also leads classes, workshops and retreats to help individuals grow personally and professionally She writes for international, national and regional magazines, and addresses corporate groups, associations, and trade conventions on the impact of appearance on individual and corporate performance. With the ability to speak five languages, Liana shares her expertise speaking and training at international speaking events. She also privately consults with major political, personal development, and business leaders on their personal and professional presence.

CONTACT

To learn more about Liana, you can go to her website, www.imagetherapists.com, where there are videos and information about her process. You can also visit www.lianasgift.com and get a beautiful gift video series on the foundation of image therapy she created. Liana is also available on social media.

CHAPTER 16:
ANNETTE LACKOVIC

"I want people to see their brilliance and leave feeling empowered to rewrite their own story."
-Annette Lackovic

Annette Lackovic ("Lack-oh-vich") is a master at arming business owners with money-making strategies and the mindset to thrive. Known as Australia's leading female sales and mindset expert, Annette is a successful speaker and trainer in high demand by Business Review Weekly (BRW) listed businesses and retail giants. Over the past 20 years, Annette has trained thousands of individuals and hundreds of companies to stay current in the marketplace by using her sales strategies.

Welcome, and thanks so much for being here, Annette.

My absolute pleasure, I'm thrilled to be doing this.

Why did you want to become a speaker? Tell us your story.

I never set out to be a speaker, it happened more organically for me. I've danced my whole life, so being on stage always felt very natural. Because I was a dancer, it was a natural progression into teaching group fitness, so I started working at a health club. The real problem I had at the time wasn't around sales or being comfortable on stage. I had always struggled with my intellect, and didn't ever think in my wildest dreams I was smart enough to speak on stage and teach people anything educational. Not until, at about age 21, I completely transformed a struggling health club that was barely making $18,000 a month into a profitable business making $68,000 a month. All within six months.

How did you manage to do that?

I did it by trying out a more natural, consultative approach to sales. Since I was 18, I had been trained in a pushy sales environment. Heavy scripting, low-integrity type of selling. We were taught to ignore the customer's questions and tell them what they need. My mantra then was, "when you tell you sell." People don't like to be sold to, but they *love* to buy. So, I wanted to create a buyer's mindset, that way my customers could feel empowered to buy and not pushed into it a sale. So, I wondered, how can we ask questions to find out a customer's needs, and just have a normal conversation?

How did you finally learn to change your approach?

One day, I put a tape recorder inside the potted plant next to where I was having a sales conversation with a lady in the health club. I wanted to analyze what I was doing so I could replicate it and train the other staff. When I listened to it, I realized I was talking about the customer's needs the entire time. I was very good at rapport building, which helps lower the customer's resistance and allows them to open up and share their challenges. Teaching the other trainers this approach made all the difference.

What a great idea. It sounds like that was a huge growth curve for you.

After that experience, I realized I wasn't 'dumb', which was the word I had always carried with me. I had a strong message to share, I could help people transform their beliefs around sales, and I wanted to help them be comfortable with selling. When I realized that I had this gift, I started training other health clubs through a training organization who shared my ethics. They also coached me on how to deliver educational workshops.

How did that change things for you?

By age 27, I started talking about the transformation that I had experienced from sales, and I was able to connect with staff members, personal trainers, and the business owners in the room who 'hadn't signed up to be sales people'. Yet they knew their business wouldn't survive without sales. I helped them understand that selling was identifying with a customer's problem, and that they were just providing a solution. That's when my speaking career really took off.

What was your next big turning point?

One day, and this was the turning point, a person I was training left the fitness industry and moved into a corporate company selling office space. He contacted me and said, "Do you train corporates?" And I thought, "I'm just going to say yes, because I'm sure that I can layer the same information over in a corporate environment." No matter what it is that you're selling, we all need to be able to extract our clients' needs, right?

How did it go?

It brought my work to a whole new level. I was able to step into a different business environment and teach people how to sell office space leasing. For me, the speaking side of my business grew rapidly. I got a referral to speak at the annual conference for what was then Australia's largest music company. Taking that gig was when I realized I was working with a scarcity mindset around money, and I needed to step up and start charging what other professionals were charging. So, I told them my speaker fee was $3000 for a 90-minute keynote, and they still wanted me! To this day, that was the most significant shift in my career.

What do you think was holding you back?

Beliefs from my family upbringing. Along with growing up in a small country town, my parents were raised just after the great depression, so a scarcity mindset was instilled in them. I guess it had trickled down to me. So, now I was charging $3,000 per speech, which was a lot for me then because I had come from always working the average wage. I started in the fitness industry at $8 per hour.

Are you still working with corporate audiences?

Yes, mostly at annual conferences. I'm in a position now where I get to pick and choose who I love to consult. It's important that I love what their product stands for. The market I've been more connected to for the past six years is the entrepreneurial market. I was drawn to work with entrepreneurs because they needed to be empowered and have a sales structure. They didn't sign up to be salespeople, they signed up to be business owners. But, learning to sell was the only way their business could survive. My speaking business in the corporate sector was easy to grow. The struggle was moving into this new market with a new audience.

How did you start to get established as a speaker in this new market?

I signed up to speak at every networking group chapter I could. I was booked at 11 chapters and allowed to give a 30-minute presentation to sell my own seminar. Out of the 11 chapters, 83 people bought my $47 ticket. Out of those 83 people, 76 turned up. This was the first event I had ever held on my own. At that moment, I realized that speaking on other people's stages was the way to grow my audience for the entrepreneurial market FAST! I'm well established today, but I was only able to get there by doing the smaller groups first. By doing that I learned how to speak to my new market. Eventually, I was noticed by bigger companies and grew a new audience and platform.

How did you initially get over your block around speaking on stage?

I continually practiced speaking, a lot. I practiced at home with pillows, believe it or not, and each pillow was an audience member. I noticed that my nerves only came if I was worried about being judged, but they'd always go away if I focused on helping that individual by connecting with their fears. One of the things that I teach, even to this day, is when you share your fears, your faults, and failures, it helps the other person feel human. To reduce their resistance, we build this unconscious level of rapport by sharing the struggles that I had with sales. They instantly feel more comfortable and empowered.

Do you ever get nervous before speaking now?

To be honest Maria, I really don't get nervous that often, only if I think I'm not prepared. Preparation is one of the best ways to overcome nerves. Sometimes I think, "I hope they like me, I hope they enjoy it." But my main focus is, "I hope that I can really shift them. I hope that I can help them step into their own brilliance and feel totally empowered." And that takes the pressure off myself. If you think about quantum physics, there's some feeling that has to come across from me to the audience. They truly know that I'm there for them, and not just to entertain. Believe me, I love to entertain as well. You can't hold the entertainer back.

What is the best way to connect and engage with an audience?

Storytelling. I cannot stress enough how important storytelling is because it creates an unconscious rapport. When done right, the audience can see themselves in the story. It humanizes you, but it's also there to teach. The story should always have a point. You can do this by sharing a fear, failure, or challenge, taking the audience through your journey and how you were able to make a breakthrough. I'm very passionate about storytelling, because it can make an impact at a deep, unconscious level. I also love to ignite the room. Having this beautiful experience of the energy shifting, and taking them on a journey. At one point they'll feel passionate, and then it may shift to sadness. Then there are times when they're laughing uncontrollably.

When we talked earlier you mentioned you were a rapper. How does that fit in?

I write a lot of music for my teachings, because it helps me deal with the challenges of being a business owner. I open or close with a song with just about every speech that I do. It makes me vulnerable and helps me connect to the audience. I'm not the best singer, and I'm not the best rapper, but I'm the only one that can share a message in that unique way. So, I add music to my presentations to give them a memorable experience, and I've noticed that it stands out and makes a difference to the audience.

How do you decide what stories to tell?

Sometimes when I'm comfortable on stage and getting ready to move into storytelling, I get this divine download of information, jokes, or stories that I wasn't planning on telling. It just comes to me. One, because I was comfortable and allowed that information to be downloaded. And two, because that's the story I can sense that they need to hear.

What do you do with your voice, body, and movement to shift the energy?

Changing volume and tone of voice creates a different energy straight away. For me, I am naturally very loud, an extrovert, and I have a lot of energy. Though, if I stayed at that high-energy level for an hour flat, it would be very tiring for the audience. So, it's important to create different intensities. Managing these in the right way ensures there is that beautiful feeling of a journey. It's like listening to an album. An album doesn't normally go 100 miles an hour for the whole album, there's always that ebb and flow of the music. It's also good to have variety in movement, with big arms and a lot of walking on stage, or sometimes just sitting still. I have a high stool on the stage, so when I go into storytelling and I want to draw the energy in, I'll always move to that stool center stage, which is a control position on a stage setup, and I'll draw the energy in purely by being still.

What's the worst thing that ever happened to you as a speaker, and how did you recover?

When I was doing training in the fitness industry, I was asked to speak at a conference, and it was the first time my numbers had jumped so high. I went from about 25 people in the room to 80, and it was a big deal for me. There were a few speakers on that day, and I was sitting in the back with one of the speakers that was on before me. She was so nervous, and I was picking up her nervous energy. I thought, "I have to walk away from her," because I've not been used to feeling these nerves and was starting to doubt myself. I was walking around and using a technique I learned from Brian Tracy to change my self-talk. And the self-talk was, "I am the best, I know my stuff, I can do it." And I was just saying this over and over again. I had this little mantra going, building myself up more and more, and I was so pumped up, Maria. I just didn't know what to do with all this energy. They called my name, I ran out to the stage and I had all this energy and was just shaking. I looked at the audience, and I just made this sound like a bird call, "Ooh-ooh-ooh-ooh-ooh-ooh". And they all just stared at me. The room was silent.

So, what happened?

The next minute I made another sound, "koo-wee!" which is like saying "Is anyone there?" And guess what they did? They made the sound right back. They laughed and thought it was part of the performance. But I was so thrown off by the whole thing, I thought, "I'll never try that again!" I certainly made an entrance.

You definitely got them engaged.

Yes. I think we're all human and can do stupid things or have horrible experiences all the time. But as soon as you shift that focus back to the audience and say, "How can I help them?" or, "What am I really here for?" you remember your intention and it helps center you and get you back on track.

How do you define success? What does that look like for you?

That's an interesting question, because I redefined it last month. After returning from my last Australian tour I realized that focusing on money is not the point of success. Doing that only created highs and lows. Now, I feel successful with helping as many people as I can to shift their mindset and believe in themselves. Being successful is empowering another individual. The more people I impact, the more successful I am. The second part of success for me is being happy. This means having time to be my own individual person. Not having to be a mom, a wife, or a teacher, but purely focused on me because that's how I show up the best. Yes, my calling is to help people change, but not just when I'm on stage. It's the ripple effect afterwards. I want people to see their brilliance and leave feeling empowered to rewrite their own story.

Getting to that clarity is such a struggle for so many speakers. Now that you've found that, how has it changed your approach with your clients and your speaking?

I'm not just about sales anymore. I know now that I'm here to make a difference through empowering people from the stage, and I teach how to do that through sales, business, and mindset. The copy I write in my blogs and my training always involves personal development. Even in one of my raps, the first line says, "Now I understand that your business is a representation of yourself," because your business will never outgrow your mindset. Your business is a replication of who you are and your values, and how you actually play. Sales and business are the two biggest personal development areas you can ever work on. You find out your fears and your blocks. People think they're coming to me for sales, and they're going to get the structures they need to build their skills. But having the mindset to do that changes everything.

What advice do you have for people who may not like to think of themselves as selling? If they're more heart-centered, or service-oriented?

You know, it's really quite funny because I don't like the word 'sales" or "selling," even though I teach it. I used to be one of those people. It wasn't until I understood that selling was just helping that I was able to fully embrace it. The purpose is to find out people's biggest challenges, fears, frustrations, concerns, and help them join the dots. That's helping. But if we were to give it a name, the name is selling. The way I help others get past that is to show them that they're offering a solution to their problem. People buy to avoid pain. More than seeking pleasure, the biggest motivator in life is the avoidance of pain. When we change our own mindset to one of helping, the customer will feel the difference and respond.

You mentioned earlier that you taught yourself how to use social media piece and speak virtually. How is that different from speaking live on stage?

Here's the thing. Nothing will ever be good enough in your own eyes. When you're recording a podcast, or speaking in front of a camera, on social media or on a live stream, you will always think could've done better. But the message, however you convey it at that time, is going to help people. I have years of early video work, and when I look back at it now I cringe. I actually wanted to remove my YouTube page and start fresh because I was so embarrassed by the videos that I recorded back in 2010. The next night, my husband sat down next to me and said, "Hey, I just got this report on the top 30 YouTube sales pages globally." And he said, "Do you know who's the top 3rd woman globally?" And I said, "No, I've got no idea." He said, "You are. You're ranked number 16 globally for the best sales training videos on YouTube." I said, "You're kidding. Yesterday I was actually thinking of wiping my whole YouTube channel."

It's a good thing you didn't.

I know, right? The second thing I've learned is to talk to the people behind the camera like they're really there. Before, I was too busy worrying about how I looked and sounded on camera, which is the same thing people do on stage. They're so busy watching themselves because they went to a speaking course, and they have to watch their "um's" and "ah's", and stand in a certain place. I understand presentation skills are important, but nothing's more important than conveying your message in the most authentic way. And the audience needs to hear your message, whether it's on camera or live.

You make it a priority to focus on the audience and make it about them and solving their problems. Do you think that's why so many people are drawn to you?

Today's world is all about individuality, and there's a specific audience that's right for you. The sooner you can connect with that audience instead of being worried about yourself, the better you'll come across. Everything that I teach is based on solving their problems. I'll look at the biggest problems people have in sales, business, or their mindset, and I'll train to that. I face things head-on and say, "Let's just get real about this, let's talk about it so we can truly help." You build a following by doing the right target marketing, and then speaking to their problems. Once you nail that, the audience will follow you.

What have you learned about working with meeting and event planners?

When you apply to speak anywhere, you need to talk about how you can add value to their organization. It's not about you wanting to speak to their audience because you're qualified and have a great business. I've seen others get rejected because their approach was more about them instead of what they could contribute to the group's audience. Focusing on adding value was a big leg up for me to grow my entrepreneurial speaking business. After doing that, I landed an amazing alliance with the largest entrepreneurial group in Australia. And, because I had such a strong message on sales and motivation, they had me go on tour. That was a huge breakthrough for me. I was able to speak on a big stage in front of my target audience, conveying a message of empowerment that I loved.

Thinking back, if you knew then what you know now, what would you have done differently?

I wish that I had believed in myself sooner, though I wouldn't be where I'm at and have the stories that I do. I'm grateful for all the learning curves, because they've made me who I am and how I'm able to help so many people.

Annette, I can't thank you enough for your time and sharing your experiences.

My absolute pleasure, Maria.

KEY TAKEAWAYS

- Selling is just identifying with a customer's problem and providing a solution.
- Step up and charge the price you're worth.
- Speak to smaller groups first and your audience will eventually grow.
- Tell stories that have a point and help build rapport with the audience.
- What's more important than presentation skills is conveying your message in an authentic way.

ABOUT ANNETTE LACKOVIC

Annette's gift is transforming people's mindset and showing them how to quickly monetize their business. Her passion is helping entrepreneurs, "make great money doing what they love by making sales easy while not feeling sleazy." Her work with her clients has generated over a billion dollars' worth of sales collectively. Along with her business and sales savvy, when Annette jumps on stage she ignites the room with her energy and singing one of her raps to help bring home the learning with a bang of entertainment.

CONTACT

You can learn more about Annette by visiting her website at www.annettelackovic.com. She has a free gift available on her website called, *The One Secret to Knowing When Your Customer is Ready to Buy,* a guide that helps you understand the invisible buying signs from your customers. Annette is also available on social media.

CHAPTER 17:
NANCY JUETTEN

"Believe and prepare as if the most important person was going to call you tomorrow."
-Nancy Juetten

Nancy Juetten (rhymes with "button") is known as the "Get Known Get Paid" mentor, and she's a powerhouse at getting speakers on the map. Nancy shows emerging speakers and coaches how to take their place on bigger live and virtual stages so they get known and paid for their brilliant work in the world. Nancy's expertise has been showcased in hundreds of prestigious media outlets including *Bloomberg Businessweek*, Fox News, and the *American City Business Journals*. She regularly contributes to many radio broadcasts, worldwide webinars, and live stages across the country.

Welcome, Nancy, thank you for joining me today.

Thanks, Maria. It's great to be here.

What led you to become a speaker? What's your story?

A number of years ago, I was working with a business coach and I told him that I was afraid to speak. He said, "Nancy, if you continue to be afraid to speak, one arm of your success will be tied behind your back. If you're happy with those odds, I'll help you to figure out other ways to grow your business. If you're ready to slay the fear and move on, I think that would be a really wise choice." I was not happy with those odds, and I decided I better slay my fears and get on with it, and so that's what I did.

That's awesome. I'm sure a lot of people resonate with that. What do you think most speakers miss today?

Often, speakers forget that people don't want more information. They want to be inspired, they want to be motivated. They want to remember what you said. When you can get out of your head, and into your heart and your gut, and tell real stories that people will remember, they will remember you.

What's the worst thing that has happened to you as a speaker?

I was invited to give a talk by a leading women's organization in Seattle, and I said, "Yes." I prepared the talk and the PowerPoint presentation. I rehearsed it in the bathroom with the hairbrush as my microphone. I thought I knew what I was doing, but I was in over my head. When I got there, I found that I was actually quite nervous, and I found that I was reading the PowerPoint, and I was not engaging with the audience. While I did the best I could, I could have done a whole lot better. My real wakeup call came when the evaluations for the speech came back from the attendees. Someone actually wrote, "I didn't pay $45 to come to a luncheon, and $10 for parking, to watch a speaker hold on to the podium for dear life, lean on PowerPoint like a crutch, and pray for the presentation to be over."

Oh, ouch.

Yeah. I'm reading this, and I'm thinking to myself, "I can either be discouraged by this and believe that I never have a career as a speaker again, or I can do whatever it takes to get better." In the years following, I took steps to get better. Last year, I got invited to speak on live and virtual stages 43 times. Every time I take the stage, it seems that I get a spinoff engagement, or a repeat engagement. If my humble beginning can be encouragement for people reading this, then I hope that it is. From humble beginnings, great things can grow.

That's inspiring. How would you advise others to get past that nervousness?

Be confident that you have what it takes to do it, and believe it in your heart, your head, and your gut. My husband has been with me on a lot of my keynote addresses. The night before, I always get nervous. He's told me before, "even the best professional basketball players that are going for the championship sometimes throw up the night before, because they are so committed to winning and serving and doing a great job." If you're feeling sick to your stomach, and like you might want to throw up, maybe that's a good sign that you really care about the audience you're here to serve. You just have to believe that the content and the message is in you.

What other advice do you have for building confidence?

Practice as often as you possibly can. If you're a reluctant speaker, you can do something as simple as set up an appointment with yourself on freeconferencecall.com. Deliver your talk into the phone, record the call, hang up the phone, and listen back to the replay. Satisfy yourself that you know this, you've got this. You can do it.

What are some thoughts you have around telling stories?

It's great to paint a picture with specific details. This activates the auditory, visual, and sensory areas of the brain. You can say something like, "When I woke up this morning, I could smell the brewing coffee. It lulled me out of my bed and into the kitchen. I was pouring the steaming coffee into my cup and thinking about how I was going to open my talk today. When I walked over to the window, I saw sheets of rain and thought to myself, 'Oh, my gosh, it's raining again. How am I going to manage my hair and get myself to the television station on time?' but here I am, and I'm so glad I'm here." Just make it real for people.

Why is telling personal stories so difficult for some people?

Vulnerability in sharing your stories is something that takes a lot of courage. But, when I tell my story about going to that women's organization and getting that horrible evaluation, it makes me relatable to the audience. If any of them have been afraid of speaking, maybe my story can help them find the courage to do it, too. The more you can lean into it, the more the audience will like and trust you, and want to hear what you say next.

How were able to move into that place of vulnerability?

I took baby steps. I'm someone who wants to get it right the first time, and I can be pretty hard on myself. I remember being in an intimate group of people, and everyone was called to stand up to share a personal story about why they do what they do. Everyone stood up and shared these bold, courageous stories. I remember feeling so much fear. I could feel tears welling up in my eyes, and I just didn't want to participate. I figured there were 27 people in the room, who's going to notice if I don't show up? Well, the facilitator of the group noticed, and when it was my turn, all eyes were on me and there was nowhere to hide.

Ooh, that's tough. So, what happened?

I remember feeling very on the spot. I said, "Listen, I'll do this, but I'm going to stay seated, because that's the best I can do." I told a very personal story that I'd never shared with anyone before. It was a pivotal moment. I shared that, as a young person in a somewhat dysfunctional family, I was never seen, heard, or celebrated for what I had accomplished. It was a deep wound in my life that was still causing me pain. That was why I was called forth to help other people be seen, heard, and celebrated for their brilliant gifts. I said that, and felt very vulnerable, but as soon as I said it, everyone in the audience rewarded me and said, "Oh my goodness, what a powerful story! You are a messenger on the path for goodness and profit, and you need to share that story more often." It was a breakthrough moment for me.

What effect did that have on you moving forward?

I learned how to step up and share even more, and do it with a little bit more confidence. It has served me well, because for a lot of us, and I learned this from Jeffrey Van Dyk, "Out of our greatest wound in life calls forth our greatest gift to share." Getting in touch with that wound and finding a way to make it a gift and service to others, can make a huge difference.

That is a brave move. What would you say to someone who's bumping up against that wall, and can't see a way to that next level?

I would invite that person to stop, look, listen, and go within. Say to her or himself, "There's something missing here. What is in my control that I can influence, so that things will feel more complete?" Speaking is a courageous profession, especially for reluctant speakers.

What are actions people can take to move through that?

If it's not going well, seek out coaches and mentors who can help you uncover a blind spot that could change everything for you. Be inspired by the speakers that move you. Keep advancing along the path to mastery by watching Ted talks and other speakers who deliver with authenticity and spirit. The more good speakers you pay attention to, the more you can emulate what's going to help you be the best that you can be.

How has speaking helped you grow your business?

Speaking on the live or virtual stage has been the single best and most reliable way to grow my tribe and my business, and build buzz around what I do. Sometimes, people just want to know you. Especially, when you're on stage, being yourself warts and all, the human reaction is instantaneous. In our world, we have telephones, multiple screens, and multitasking. When you're in front of a room full of real people, they have to pay attention. When you're doing a webinar or teleclass, sometimes people do them while they're jogging, or doing 42 other things. When you're in front of real people, the intimacy and the connection that you can make when you show up is unparalleled, and I think it took me a really long time to embrace that.

How is live speaking different from speaking virtually? Are there certain things I need to do differently?

With virtual speaking, you need to look into the camera as though you're looking at one specific person, like your BFF, or your ideal client. Sometimes that's very uncomfortable for people, so practice if you can. Something you can do is use Be Live TV or your smart phone, and you can record a video. Just look into the little red dot, then upload the video to YouTube and see how it looks. Watch it back and notice, am I actually looking into the camera? Do I look like I'm having fun? Do I look like I'm connecting with my BFF? If it doesn't look like you are, delete the video and try again. If you're doing virtual training or speaking, make sure you're in an attractive environment where what the viewer doesn't see a messy desk, with a busy bulletin board. Create a tranquil, optimistic, success-reflective environment, so when people see you, you look like the rock star that you are.

Those are great tips. How do you have an authentic, emotional connection, as if there were a live audience there, when you're staring at a screen?

Choose your words as if you're talking to one person, "Thank you for joining me today." Instead of saying, "Thank you everyone for being here, there are folks calling from all around the world. Talk to them like there's only one person. Let them know there's some intimacy and connection, "I'm really glad you made today's call a priority, I promise I'm going to pour massive value into this training and give you more than I ever thought possible, so this time that we are spending together is well worth it." Let people know that you're committed to serving at a very high level, and that this will be very well worth their time.

That's great advice. Selling is something that all of us are doing all the time, even if we're just trying to sell our idea. What tips would you have around selling?

Start the presentation with the end in mind. Recognize how much time you've been given, so that you use the time wisely. If you only have 15 or 20 minutes on the stage, that's probably not enough time to do a full-blown offer, where you describe all the bells and whistles of your delicious, juicy program that's going to change their lives. In 20 minutes, you can probably use 15 minutes to create "know-like trust," tell two stories that make your points, and then say, "If you love what you've heard so far, and you know that I could be the guide to get you to the next level, I want you to know that I have made a couple of appointments available, so that we can actually talk and see if I might be the guide to get you there. If that interests you, come and see me, and we'll get you on the calendar. It's been my pleasure to speak with you today, thank you very much."

What would it look like if you had more time?

If you have a longer period of time, and the host has said it's all right for you to make an offer, allow for enough time, and make a seamless transition from your storytelling to your offer. That typically means you want to share three compelling reasons why making a shift is going to be powerful. Then you want to shift into a statement, which would be something like, "The trouble is, getting rid of these problems is something that keeps people awake at night, and it keeps them worried and concerned, and as a result of that, they struggle and continue to have difficulty for a lot longer than they want to. That's why I, as the expert in X Y Z, have devoted my life to helping slay that problem at the cellular level. If it's okay with you, I'd like to tell you more about how I could help you more deeply." Then you can move into how you're going to invite them into a program that will solve their urgent problem. By recognizing how much time you have, and using the time wisely, you can accomplish the end that you had in mind and earn the rewards of a happy audience.

I really like how you're inviting the audience. You ask for permission.

I love the idea of inviting people and asking permission. Not long ago I did one of these 20 minute talks, and I gave the vulnerable story, and a couple of juicy tips, and a couple of great examples, and right about the 12-minute mark, I asked the audience, "How's it going so far? Are you getting some real value? Are you having some fun? Are you feeling like this was a good investment of your $45 and your $10 for parking?" Everybody said, "Yes, I'm loving it." So, there's an opportunity for me to say, "Well, if you're loving it, I want you to know that I teach a course called the *Attract Ideal Clients and Speaking Gigs at Hello Success Training*, and one lucky member of today's audience is going to be invited in as a VIP guest when you all decide to enter to win this scholarship. If this is of interest to you, it's a $997 value. I've got a business card basket right here. If that serves you, go ahead and put your name in the basket." Then I went ahead and told my final story. When the basket was delivered to me, 100% of the people in the room had put their names in. I asked the host, "Would you do me the honor of pulling the name out of the basket, and choosing the name of our winner?" The person just jumped out of her chair like she'd won the lottery, and we had a hug, and it was beautiful.

What happened after that?

I had people coming to the back table saying, "You know that thing she won? I want to buy that." I only had 20 minutes, but I used it as an opportunity to grow my community by inviting people to step into something of value that they wanted. It also gave me the opportunity to see what would serve that audience best. What do you know? They got what they wanted, I got what I wanted, and now we're journeying forward together.

Do you sometimes have people that don't want to participate?

Sure. Not everyone joins the list, or enters to win. I always say, if you don't want to stay in touch with me, cross your e-mail address off that business card, and I will honor that. I go through the business cards and I see how many people have scratched off their e-mail address, and none of them have. I know that I serve them. As I stay in touch with them with my newsletter and other things, invariably people raise their hand when the time is right, and they say, "You know that program you talked about at that event we went to? Can I start now?" "Of course you can. I can't wait to serve you." That's how I do things when I only have 20 minutes. It works pretty well for me, it may work for you too.

You've been a successful publicist. What would you suggest for people as they're thinking about how to put this together? Is there a certain formula or secret tips to do that?

Well, I do have a secret, ninja tip. Sometimes, we go to networking events and big events, we meet a lot of people and we ask, "What do you do?" They say, "I'm a professional speaker." Well, if you're in a room full of professional speakers, just calling yourself a professional speaker does not get you invited to speak. You haven't differentiated yourself. I highly recommend that you prepare a speaker sheet that says, "I am a motivational keynote speaker." Make it clear how awesome you are in the third person, so that when you look at that, you know what you talk about. You know how the audience benefits. You know how other people have responded to your message, and you are ready to go. You don't get invited to speak unless you have a sassy topic to talk about that has three compelling takeaway points that the audience will be made better for having enjoyed. When you have this, you can pitch yourself to any organization that's the right fit for your message. Then follow-up, get yourself booked on that stage, and have the perfect audience waiting to benefit from what you have to offer.

What do you say to people who don't have their speaker sheet ready?

If you don't have that, you may be wishing and hoping that the phone would ring, and when the phone rings, you trip, because you're not ready. Behave and believe as if the most important person was going to call you tomorrow, and that you have your message under your thumb right this very minute. When you do, big, huge doors open, and you get to walk through them with grace and ease as opposed to having that 11th hour scramble, where you're going to say something like, "I can speak about a variety of things in a variety of ways, and I can't wait to be of service", which says absolutely nothing.

So many people fall into that trap.

Oh, my gosh, cry me a river. I see it every single day. You need to answer, "What is specific and terrific about my talk that sets me apart from everyone else?" Then create a speaker sheet that shares your topic and three takeaway points. Once you have that, your job is to romance those three takeaway points.

How do you do that?

You answer three questions. What is the point? Why does it matter? How can I apply it? The trouble is that most people struggle getting this into their heart, their head, and their bones, which is why I have devoted my life to helping people solve this problem. Here's what you can ask: "Would it be okay with you if I invited you to take a look at something that could help ease this for you?" Then you ease into the pictures and the benefits and how people can buy it. That would be a structure that would work pretty well for most people. You need to get ready with the big pieces first. What do you talk about? How will the audience benefit? Why you? And, how can they book you?

Once they have that, what advice do you have for people who are ready and want to get booked? How do they do that?

I have a real-life example that I can share. It had been a year since I led a big webinar, and I wanted to give it everything I had. I decided to host a webinar, and talk about the three best ways you can get booked on more live and virtual stages, even if you're not the most known speaker. I had three takeaway points and a bonus tip that was going to change everything. What do you know? 1500 people around the world came to this webinar. I delivered this self-hosted webinar like it was the most important presentation of my life. When the phone hit the cradle, and I completed my event, within a week, I had been invited to give that same talk to 10 additional audiences of my perfect people.

Wow.

You don't know who's listening to your event. If you deliver a workshop and invite the right people to come, and you rock that stage and serve that audience, someone is going to say, "Wow that was awesome. I want to refer you to three other places where you can give that same talk." That will boost your confidence big time.

Thinking back, if you knew then what you know now, what would you have done differently?

If I had it to do over again, I would have done more live speaking sooner, instead of hiding behind my computer, trying to get things perfect. I would stop trying to be like other people, and step into who I am sooner. If I had done those things, there would probably be a couple of extra zeros to my income today. But, I cannot cry in my beer for my journey, because here I am these many years later. The speed with which my business has grown, the amount of opportunities I now have to speak on live stages, is head-spinning. I've been humbled by my experiences and without too much attachment to what result will flow, I just try to be the best I can be and know the right things will happen.

Beautiful. Thank you for your time today. Do you have any final messages or takeaways?

I just want to thank you for the opportunity to share this message. When you put your head down, and your heart in it, you will get there. You'll touch a lot of lives. Go live as soon as possible, in front of real people. Today, with Facebook Live, and Be Live TV, and other kinds of resources, you can deliver your message around the globe just from your computer. Don't be reluctant to show up, even though it's scary. It's wasted time and lost economy to try to get perfect. What people really want is the real you. That's why I say, "embrace your quirks, raise your voice, inspire, and lead, because if not now, then when?"

Nancy, thank you for being here and sharing your story.

Thanks for the opportunity, Maria.

KEY TAKEAWAYS

▸ Tell real stories that people will remember and they will remember you.

▸ Be confident that you have what it takes.

▸ Practice as much as you can.

▸ Learn to be vulnerable, it makes you relatable to the audience.

▸ When speaking to a camera, make it intimate and speak to just one person.

ABOUT NANCY JUETTEN

Luminaries, including Alex Mandossian, Sandra Yancey, Loral Langemeier, and Christine Kloser are among Nancy's clients. Her Sizzling Speaker Sheet template, systems, and natural talent with marketing messaging guide her fans, clients, and followers to attract more of their ideal clients and speaking gigs at "hello." Joint venture partners in the transformational coaching industry describe her as a Joint Venture Leaderboard Topping Angel because she frequently delivers credible influence that drives sales for her partners and commissions to her mailbox.

CONTACT

To learn more about Nancy, you can visit her website at www.GetKnownGetPaid.com. Nancy has a free gift called, "The Sizzling Speaker Sheet" that will help you get ready to take the stage as soon as possible. You can find it at www.sizzlingspeakersheet.com. You can reach out to Nancy by e-mail at Nancy@GetKnownGetPaid.com, and she is on social media.

CHAPTER 18:
DARREN TAY

Darren Tay is the first person from Singapore to win the Toastmaster World Championship of Public Speaking. He is a 27 year-old lawyer and the world's #1 champion in public speaking. Darren launched his first book, *Express To Impress*, in 2012, which became the Bestselling book in Singapore. Darren is the Managing Director and Master Trainer of the Public Speaking Academy, a company he founded in 2009. Since then, he has been a nine-time national public speaking champion.

Welcome, and thanks for being here Darren.

Thank you so much for having me.

You've accomplished a lot in your 27 years and I'd like to back up and hear how you got to where you got to where you are today. How did you get started in public speaking?

When I began public speaking, I did not quite like the experience. I was 14 years old and still a very shy and reserved individual. What launched me was when my English language teacher gave me an ultimatum. She said, "Enough is enough Darren. You can no longer hide behind the screens and just design the PowerPoint slides. You have to take the foreground." So, she said, "If you don't speak for this important project, I'm going to fail you for the English Language paper." In Singapore if you fail the English Language paper, no matter how well you do in other classes, you fail automatically for the entire year. I took that seriously.

Wow. I think I would, too.

I can still remember my presentation today. It was a book review on Harry Potter and the Sorcerer's Stone. I rehearsed at least 20 to 30 times the night before the presentation. On the day of the presentation, I'll never forget what the teacher said right after my presentation. She faced the entire class and said, "Class, this is how you should all present next time." That one statement of affirmation from the teacher changed my life. But she did not stop there. The next day she asked whether I would be keen to present the same book review at the school library. She designed posters, *Watch Darren Tay do a live book review, Harry Potter and the Sorcerer's Stone* and posted it all over the school, even in the school toilets. You can imagine how disturbing it was for students to go to the rest room and see my face there! That was how my speaking career started and I'm really thankful to her.

Isn't it amazing how much impact one person can have on our entire lives?

You're absolutely right.

Congratulations. You're the 2016 #1 World Champion Toastmaster! You've done a lot of public speaking, but were you nervous for this? What was it like?

To be honest, I was very nervous for the presentation, especially when I went into the grand finals. There were ten speakers and about 1,600 individuals watching, with many more watching worldwide, so I was really concerned. I was wondering whether the audience members would be with me, would they be laughing at my punch-words and punchlines, and would I fumble on stage? Right then my coach reminded me, "If the focus is on you, it's not the right focus." My mom also referenced a quote, "Instead of thinking of it as a competition, just imagine you had seven minutes and 30 seconds of the world's time… what message would you give to the world?" That helped calm my nerves. I did my absolute best that day.

That was great advice they gave you. What would you say to those people who have a hard time getting over being nervous?

I think most speakers have the wrong idea about getting nervous. So many individuals have fear thinking, "Oh, why are there butterflies in the stomach?" Because often we're told the goal is that we should get rid of the anxiety, we should get rid of the butterflies in the stomach. We can't get rid of the butterflies in our stomach. Anxiety is part of being human, so instead of trying to get rid of the butterflies, the goal is to make those butterflies fly in formation.

What do you mean by that?

It is possible to change the relationship that you have with anxiety. If you ask some of the best speakers, whether it's Barack Obama or Steve Jobs, how they feel prior to taking the stage, they feel butterflies in their stomach too, but they do it anyway. Tony Robbins says it best, "When you feel nervous, when you feel fearful, especially for speaking or taking a particular cause of action, know that we all feel fear. I feel fear as well, but I just do it anyway." I recommend using the right breathing techniques, along with a mindfulness practice. Another technique is to adopt a 'power pose' and there's a well-known TED Talk on power poses, and how to use them to help increase your confidence. And finally, visualization. So often we let our minds wander off and picture a negative result, rather than visualizing things working out smoothly. Imagine the talk happening perfectly, feeling completely confident on stage, the people's faces in the audience, and everyone clapping at the end.

So, what do you do to get your butterflies in formation?

Rehearsal is extremely important, but instead of just rehearsing in front of the mirror I videotape my performances and then show it to some of my friends, my coach and mentors to get feedback. I also practice mindfulness meditation. Mindfulness meditation helps calm my nerves whenever I feel anxious prior to going on stage to speak. I am able to get in tune with the physical sensation of my body, see things in perspective and change my relationship with anxiety.

That's wonderful. Do you do that every time you speak?

Yes, every time I speak and throughout my day. I meditate ten minutes when I wake up and ten minutes before going to bed.

And how has that changed your life?

It has changed a lot, not just for my speaking endeavors but in dealing with everyday life. When I was about 18 years old, going through a major national examination, I was really stressed out, and I was thinking, "This is a make or break moment," and my mind started to worry about the future, and what would happen if I didn't do well. In doing that, I missed out on the present. I realize now that mindfulness helps me stay centered, rooted, and anchored in the present moment. Whenever there's an anxious feeling, instead of resisting or fighting it, I am now able stay with it and see it. That is changing your relationship with anxiety, and it has changed my whole perspective in life.

I love that. And that's great advice, recording yourself and then reviewing it. What other tips do you have for rehearsing and improving?

When people play back and review the video recordings there are three steps. First, 'visuals only', where you mute the audio.

You just simply watch and observe your body language, notice if you rotate your hips or start swaying from the left to right. Observe your facial expressions as well as your movements and stage positioning. Second, play the audio only. Don't watch yourself, just listen. Listen to your diction and pronunciation, your volume, pitch and speed. And finally, play the video along with audio. Look at the whole picture, and evaluate how your presentation looks and sounds.

When you look at the big picture, how do you go about coming up with your core message? Do you talk about the same message or do you have a number of different talks you do?

I have a number of different talks. And to help individuals come up with a core message, first come up with a list of topics you feel very strongly about. Look at the topics and ask yourself which one you feel the strongest about and most drawn to. Then test it out before a live audience. Because at the end of the day, we can't talk about a message that does not resonate with them.

And what is the common feeling or theme that tends to be in all the different speeches you give?

The common element is authenticity. I've spoken on different topics and genres, but I speak from my own experience. I speak about pursuing your dreams and how I overcame the odds by becoming a successful entrepreneur at 20. I speak about dealing with stress and anxiety and that the solution is getting in tune with your body and living in the now. I also speak about dealing with internal and external bullies. All of these have one central thread that strings them together and it's uniquely Darren Tay.

Let's look at the different types of speaking. Describe how the Toastmaster process is different from other types of speaking, like a keynote or corporate training.

In Toastmasters, I love the nurturing and learning environment. People are very supportive, encouraging and may even give you a standing ovation. The Toastmasters process is a peer-evaluation environment, with someone who has more speaking experience to give you feedback. There is a structure and timing for an individual to deliver the speech: 1-2 minutes 30 seconds for impromptu, or 5-7 minutes 30 seconds for a prepared speech. The difference in delivering a keynote or doing a corporate training is that we have the time and luxury to customize a learning program with opportunity to engage the audience and practice.

You did such a great job in your Toastmaster grand finals presentation blending your powerful message with humor, and building curiosity with the "prop" that you had. Is that what you call it?

Yeah.

How did you learn to pull all of those things together, with a powerful message and humor?

It took 13 years of experience in speaking, training, and failing many times, before I discovered the techniques that would work to engage the audience. When I first started, I was told two important principles for public speaking. One, it's important to incorporate humor, because it helps lower the defensiveness of the audience. You can instantly establish rapport, especially when you have such a short time to expose yourself. Number two is to tell a story, because we know that "facts tell, stories sell." But, for this to be true, you must tell the story *well*. Use dialogue and take on the personas of the characters in the story. That makes it much more real. Bring your audience members into the story by reenacting the scene. Props go a long way to help the audience visualize what's going on. The prop I used was arguably a risky move and I will leave it to the readers to google it and see what the prop was, to keep the element of surprise.

What advice would you have for people on how to pull in the right stories in your talk, ones that draw people in but also relate to the point you're making?

For storytelling, we follow a narrative curve, where we build up the tension, then get to the climax before sharing the resolution. There are techniques involved in crafting a story that make people laugh, bring them on an emotional rollercoaster ride, and make them feel like they're a part of the story. Start a story bank, a place to start if you've never captured your stories. You can use your mobile phone to create a document or a notes page and then write down ideas for stories wherever you go. Add them to the list so it's easy to find and pull out relevant stories when you need them. The real test is to tell the story to a live audience, because sometimes we think that a story will resonate, and then it falls flat. But that can provide valuable insights on to how to improve the story, either the content or the delivery.

Think back to all the times you've spoken. What's the worst thing that has happened, and how did you recover?

When I'm about to deliver a punchline or a punch-word I first set it up to create the element of surprise. The worst thing that happened to me was on stage, as I was setting up my punch-word. I remembered the setup but I forgot the punch-word. I was flustered, thinking through the lines, trying to remember all the pieces leading up to it. I did number one and number two, those as the setup, and number three would be the punch-word, and I forgot what it was! So instead of fumbling on stage and saying, "Oh sorry, let me repeat it," or just pausing, I moved ahead. I just went through it, as if that wasn't an intentional part for me to make the audience members laugh. I was quite taken by surprise, but I just gave another word that somehow matched that trio and the audience members laughed anyway, so it turned out okay.

You seem to have a lot of fun when speaking, and humor is such an important way to connect with the audience. What's it like for you when you're speaking? Are you having fun?

Yeah. I enjoy it a lot. I like sharing the message and it feels very satisfying when the audience laughs along with you. It feels great when they react, get engaged, or ask questions at the end. So, I really enjoy taking the stage, but that wasn't the case when I started at age 14. It was a very traumatic experience because I had anxiety around whether I would perform well and whether the audience members would laugh. Over the years, as I trained myself and received advice from mentors and coaches, I learned how to shift my focus off myself and over to the audience. The audience clearly benefits when I present from that perspective.

Many speakers don't begin until much later than 27. What would you say to younger or more inexperienced people when they're starting out?

I used to have think that you need to be born a talented public speaker. I realized over the years that it's a skill that can be learned. It all depends on the level of investment you put into it with time, effort and training/coaching. My mantra is always 'nurture over nature'. I've often showed a video of me speaking at age 14. Most of the audience members would be like, "Oh my goodness, that's so terrible." The longest five minutes of my life! But here I am now, a world champion in speaking. So, I would say, "If I did it, so can you." Second, it's like cycling and swimming. You cannot learn it just by watching a video on YouTube or reading a book. You have to do it. Grab opportunities to speak, whether it's in class, on stage, at work, or outside with friends in an interpersonal communication setting. But go out there and speak. The best way to accelerate your learning curve exponentially is to videotape yourself speaking, and then play it back as I described earlier. The sooner the better. It takes a lot longer to erase bad habits than to build the right ones early on.

Many people focus on the message and the speech and forget that they're performing and need to use the stage and their body. What insights can you share around this?

It depends on the size of the stage. If it's large, then your body language needs to be amplified. There are also key techniques with your nonverbals. The first is stage positioning and the second is hand gestures. With stage positioning, the general rule is, as you move, you speak. Moving around without speaking looks awkward. You also need to know from which side of the stage you will be moving. If you are going through a chronological event, then move from left to the right, because most people read from left to the right. Also, many speakers gesture at the wrong level of the body. Some do it very high, at the chest level or sternum. When you do that your shoulders naturally raise and it makes you look tense. So, drop your shoulders and gesture at the bellybutton area. Just imagine yourself in a swimming pool with the water up to your waist. Make sure when you use gestures, your hands are not dipped in the water. Also, move your hands further away from your body. That allows the audience to better see your hand gestures.

As I watched your talk, I noticed that you use dramatic and powerful pauses to let certain statements just soak in. What's your advice on how to do this well?

Many people are fearful of pausing because they associate pausing with forgetting your lines, trying to recall what you're gonna say next. When individuals pause while looking upwards or downwards, it indicates they're trying to recall a certain part of the speech or what they're going to say next. The best way to pause is to make sure that you sustain eye-contact. If you pause while maintaining eye-contact it will show the audience members that you are pausing deliberately. Another technique is to make sure that you use your voice. Play around with the speed, the volume and the pitch. If you are trying to deliver a very important message or punchline, then just prior to that, slow down and get softer.

What do you think is unique about you as a speaker?

I think my greatest strength lies in my energy and my dynamic body language. It's about matching the audience members' energy level first, and then slowly bringing them to the place I want them to be. I don't start off by immediately making a huge impact. I will start with maybe a pause or by scanning the crowd, and reading the audience. For my keynotes or workshops I mingle with the participants first so I know where they're at.

Do you have a chance before most keynotes to find out who is in the audience, and if not, what advice do you have for people on how to read them as soon as you walk onto the stage?

Sometimes I don't have the opportunity of speaking with audience members. If I know that in advance, then I contact the organizers and ask for a brief description of the audience. Where they're from, their background, their organizations, and some common stories or experiences that they share. I also check what speeches they have heard so far, so that I can incorporate my examples in a way that's new and relates to them. The moment I hit the stage, I smile and the beautiful thing is when there is a mirroring effect from the audience. When I give a bright, genuine and beautiful smile, many of them smile back and that helps to calm my nerves. It also helps prepare the audience and get them thinking, "Hey this speaker is ready, this speaker is here to share with us his experiences and speak to us authentically."

How do you immediately engage them and grab their attention? What is your process for opening your talk?

I first run through what I'm going to do in the back of my mind. If it's a keynote I will start quite differently from a workshop. For a keynote, I engage the audience members with a survey, and get them to participate by raising their hands. This gives me a sense of how they feel and their thoughts on certain issues. Sometimes, I have them do an activity right at the start. I'll walk offstage onto the floor and get them involved in an exercise where they have to stand up or participate. As far as walking on stage, staying planted, staying rooted, I don't think you should just start rattling off the moment you take the stage, but instead walk right to the middle of the stage. Sometimes I will start with an opener that I rehearsed to get them thinking.

How did you build all the different parts to your business, and what would you recommend to others on how to expand into other areas?

You need to be very clear on what you want as a client. Most speakers operate with a marketing funnel. It just depends on how clear and effective that marketing funnel is. The goal is to pull ideal prospects into your funnel so they can become clients. You start out by providing a lead magnate or freebie for the audience members to "opt in," whether it's a free book, free tips or a free video. Then afterwards, you invite them to a free preview, like a webinar or teleseminar. After that, you share an opportunity for them if they would like to find out more. If they are keen to find out more, they can sign up for your program, which has greater value and requires payment.

What if you have other things that you want to offer?

There are some individuals who want a customized program with a personal touch and are willing to pay a premium for it. That is where they go further into the marketing funnel for the premium one-to-one coaching. It's important to have a clear roadmap in mind (training, keynotes, workshops, groups programs, etc.), so you can decide which activities you want to do at what time. You can eventually do all of them, provided you know when to pursue which activity. It's best to start out with just one or two areas and build them up first.

What would you say to people who are hesitant to offer something through their talk?

There are two main issues here. That first one is whether they see value in their own product, and second is the psychological barrier they have in seeing themselves as a selling speaker, and doing what we call the direct or 'hot sales'. When it comes to speaking, there are two elements. First is the substance, and second is the marketing. There are some speakers who have great substance and content, and deliver great value, but they have no idea how to market themselves. Those are speakers who aren't able to convert their fans into clients. There are also individuals who have great marketing skills but hardly any substance. Those people may be able to get the first wave of clients in, but after that, they're probably not going to have recurring customers. The speaker we want to be is one with substance that can offer great value and knows how to market themselves really well.

How does someone change their thinking around this?

Don't start with a premise of how much money you can make from the audience, but with how much value you can give them. This is where back of the room sales, the marketing funnel, and doing what we call 'pitches' come in, and those require training and practice. Today, selling is about pre-framing the audience before you even begin your presentation, and before you move into the last segment of talking. Maybe your program has great value but if you don't help *them* see the value then it's going to be difficult. There are many techniques to do this, like sharing a testimonial, or showing the benefits the audience will get and how their lives will improve. Because it's not really about the money. They want to know what return they're getting and when they can expect that return.

If you knew then what you know now, what would you have done differently?

If I knew then what I know now, what would I have done differently? Hmm. This is a very intriguing question. This is lovely. What would I do differently? I would change my mindset around investing in a mentor or coach. With the knowledge that I have now, the number one thing that I would change would be to go with the investment as soon as possible. My advice is whether it's for free or for a fee, get a mentor, because that's going to accelerate your learning curve. Investing in yourself is one of the best investments you can make.

Darren, I can't thank you enough for your time and sharing such great takeaways.

Thank you so much, Maria! You've been an inspiration to all in coming up with this beautiful endeavor. I wish you the very best.

KEY TAKEAWAYS

‣ Great speaking is a skill that can be learned.

‣ Invest early in a mentor, coach, or training to get to the level you need.

‣ Anxiety is part of being human, so instead of trying to get rid of the butterflies, make the butterflies fly in formation.

‣ Videotape yourself speaking. Observe only, then listen only, then watch the entire video.

‣ Tell a story, because "facts tell, stories sell," but for this to be true, you must tell the story well.

ABOUT DARREN TAY

Darren has made several media appearances and was a celebrity speaker and judge on the national Chinese TV program, Star Hub. He is an inspiration to kids worldwide, spreading the message that excellence in effective communication can be achieved with the right techniques and strategies.

CONTACT

Visit Darren's website, www.darrentay.com to request his free gift, *The Five Tips of the World Champion of Public Speaking,* and his book "Express to Impress." His academy website is: www.publicspeakingacademy.com.sg. Darren uploads new videos to his YouTube channel weekly, is available on social media. Email Darren at: darrentay@publicspeakingacademy.com.

CHAPTER 19:
BARBARA CHURCHILL

"Let me be the vehicle for this message so that they hear it in the way that they need to hear it today."
-Barbara Churchill

Barbara Churchill is a sought-after leadership coach, specializing in emerging and senior level women leaders as well as women entrepreneurs. She is passionate about empowering women to embrace their leadership skills and step into more challenging roles. As a dynamic, high energy, and engaging speaker who mixes humor with a powerful message, Barbara has been mentoring working women for over 20 years. Having built and run three successful businesses herself with revenues in seven figures, she's learned what it takes to create the kind of work-life balance that's meaningful and sustainable.

Welcome, Barbara. It is so wonderful to be with you today.

Hey, Maria. Nice to be here. Good to talk to you.

When and how did you first step into speaking?

Speaking wasn't really a passion that I chose to pursue. It was more about getting my message to women because of my coaching practice. I kept seeing the same things over and over. Whether they were brand-new to leadership, a senior or executive level, or small business owners like myself, women leaders kept presenting with the same issues. I thought, "Darn it anyway. I have got to get out there and let women know about these issues, how we can deal with them, and how we can gain more confidence and communicate more effectively." I kind of just fell into it. I'd have a client, and they'd ask, "Hey, can you come into our organization and speak to our women's leadership group?" Or, "Hey, we're having a conference coming up and your topic would be really great." It was all based on referral.

People come into speaking from such different angles. You were helping women through coaching and training, and the referrals from that pulled you into the speaking.

Yeah, and I love that the women I coach have a collaborative mindset, so it wasn't about competition. It was, "Oh, I know so many women who are struggling with this and that, so let's bring you in here," or, "Could you possibly contact this person?" I loved that about workshops, but then I thought to myself, you know, there's got to be a larger scale that I could do this on, because I'm all about, as you are, how can I bring multiple streams of income into my business? That's where the speaking bug got me, and it was a natural fit. I am kind of a ham, I'm going to just say. I like to have a microphone.

I know. We all do, right? How did you build up those skills and make an entree into speaking?

I come from a theatrical family. My sister and I were in theater when we were kids. My children have been active in high school and college theater. So, I thought, I've got to start to rehearse. Where can I go to get in front of people all the time? I thought Toastmasters would be a great start for two reasons. One, you craft a very quick speech. It really helps you hone your message, because you have just a short window of time to make an impact. Speeches are typically five to seven minutes, so I thought, "Yeah, I'm gonna start with Toastmasters, just so I can get the practice."

What else do they do in Toastmasters?

They do things like table topics, where you're asked a question, and then you speak extemporaneously for one to two minutes. I love to do off-the-cuff, and I am pretty good at that, but I'm a big believer in honing the skillset that you already have and diving deep. Instead of going wide, I like to go really deep, so Toastmasters was a great fit for me. I started with that, and I would try to do some kind of speaking every single week.

What was your approach when first starting out?

I started asking to speak at rotary clubs, women's groups, networking groups, chamber groups, not to get paid because I had a thriving coaching and facilitation retreat practice, but just to get out there and see. It's a very different animal to do a workshop than a keynote speech. There are a lot of people that say, "Oh, I love to speak. I think I'd be a really great speaker." That may be the case, but you have to know the nuances of the types of speaking. In a workshop, you can really connect with people. You're in the room with them, same level, walking around. When you're doing a keynote speech for 1,500, 5,000 people, you don't have that same ability to be with them in terms of their particular space, but you have to make that same connection, so it's a very different feel.

How do you move from one to another? How do you prepare differently for the different audiences?

It's so important for the keynote audience to walk away with an experience. I don't want them to walk away and say, "Yeah, that was entertaining," and then be left with nothing. "What did she talk about? I don't know but she was funny." That's not a success for me. I want to give them three takeaways, no more than three, and I want to dive deep into that. In training, you could do a half-day workshop. In a keynote, you've got 45, maybe 90 minutes, to have them there with you, and you want to bring them through this experience. It's like a story arch, and you have much more story than you do training or education. You have your points, and then you illustrate each point with a story.

How do you approach your stories? Everybody seems to do it a little bit differently.

I'm big on rehearsal. Yes, they're my stories and people kind of tend to lean back on their elbow and say, "Oh, my gosh. It's my story, so of course I can tell it." But, there is a craft to good storytelling, and I rehearse a lot. I have taken courses on how to be a better storyteller. I'm a big believer in professional development. I can't tell you how many courses I've taken over the 20 plus years I've been in business, because I want to keep getting better and better, and because I want the experience for my audience to be getting better and better. I want them to walk away and say, "Wow. Did you hear Barbara Churchill? Not only is she funny, but here's what she talked about. Boom, boom, boom." That's a success for me, when they walk away feeling good, and they've got actionable items they can do.

What would be the top two, three things to keep in mind about how to tell a story?

You want to keep it really tight. When you have a point, the story needs to match the point. You want to bring people in and have some drama. It's like a little mini-theater. You want them to be drawn into what you're saying, and how it's pertinent to your point. They've got to match. I'm sure people have been in keynote speeches thinking, "How is this related to what this guy is talking about?"

What's the best way to pull together a talk?

I think rehearsal is key. Rehearse and learn how to craft a great story. I'm big on bullet points. I used to script things out, and then you get into this memorizing thing. I've been on stage and all of a sudden, my presentation goes to screensaver, and I have absolutely no idea what's coming next, and I say, okay. Here is the time to wing it. If you have memorized it and you have that problem, then you don't know what's next. So, I've gone to bullets. If you give me bullets, then I'm good. And this is where rehearsal comes in.

Coming from your theater background, what thoughts can you share with people about the performance?

Imagine yourself at a cocktail party, and somebody is telling you a really good story. You're just so engaged in it, right? What's happening? What's that person doing? They are using facial expressions. They're over-animating. They use hand gestures. They may be imitating how somebody walks. They will use different inflections on their voice. They'll get very loud at the dramatic parts and then they come in to really bring you into it. There are all kinds of things that you can learn that will make storytelling much more entertaining, and it will engage your audience. It will bring them into the experience because that's what you want. You want them to feel what you felt. You want them to understand and be in that moment with you. There are so many people who think, I have to make them cry. No, you don't. You have to make them care about what you're talking about. As far as hand gestures, remember you're going to be in front of a big group, and people are in the back. They can't see you, so use the space. We are not people that use our bodies in our spaces very well. Really over-emphasize, and if you think you're doing it too flamboyantly, I'll guarantee you aren't.

People usually think they're loud enough, and often they're not.

No, and we rely on our microphone, so you need to get really engaged. It's about getting outside of your comfort zone. There's that voice in our head that says, "No, no, no. You don't want to do that. Don't take the risk." Don't listen to that voice. You have to really get out there and it is an exposure. You are in front of people, being who you are, and there's a certain risk in terms of exposure there. If you know your content, and you're passionate about that, and you're there to enlighten, empower, inspire, what is your purpose? People will feel that and they will get you. In my opinion, perfection has nothing to do with speaking, because if I go out there and I am absolutely perfect, will I be relatable? What's more important for me is to be relatable. I want them to go, "Wow, I'm just like her, or I had that experience, and she handled it this way. I bet I could, too."

How did you get to know your message, what you were good at, and really hone that brand so that it pulled people in?

I think that's a great question. I'm a big believer in just being who I am. I have had years of experience not doing that. We have these voices, I call them your outside critics, telling you their perspectives and their perceptions. You've really got to think to yourself, "How do I want to show up in the world? Who do I want to be? Who is my real self?" I want to be as authentic as I can be, so I say this is who I am, and if you like me, that's fine. I'm not attached to it. If you don't, that's okay too, because we're not going to be liked by everybody.

That's a great mindset.

Here's my thing. Regardless of whether you liked how I present, did you get the message? If so, then I'm good. So, I detach from worrying if they are going to love me or not. You can really have a crisis of confidence if all you're looking for is the applause. I don't care if it's to 30 people or 3,000 people. My brand is just, how are you? You're my friend. Welcome to my living room. This stage right here, this is my space. I'm so glad you could come over. Let's talk a little bit and have a conversation. That's how I want to feel.

What style do you go for when presenting?

I don't wear jeans. I don't wear suits. That's just not my thing. I wear dresses. I wear what I like. I don't wear what I think I should based on someone else's opinion. I dress for what I like. I have more of an upscale brand because that's the level of people that I work with. It just feels right. When we start branding ourselves like someone else or how we think we're supposed to, then we're being a copycat, and we're not being ourselves. It might be incongruent with who you really are, and it's going to show. It's going to show in your blogging. It's going to show in your speaking. You're going to feel it in your body, and you're going to wonder, "Why isn't this working?" I recommend just be you, because we need your voice. We need your perspective. There are no new ideas. I'm just going to tell you. If you look at what's out there in terms of personal development, personal brand, it's all kind of the same stuff, just packaged in different ways. Package it in a way that resonates with you, because your people will find you.

If your goal is to have everyone like you, you're going to fail because you'll be going from one persona to the next, trying to find the one that lands to get everyone to like you, and you're not going to get it.

Plus, it sets you up for disappointment. If all you're looking for is the applause, that isn't a good business model. What is your message? What is the purpose of what you do? Why are you doing this? What do you want to achieve by this? If it's to be liked, then just perform for family and friends. If it's to get a message across, then let's get to the meat of that, and who cares about the likeability factor. Let's get the message across.

What is your advice around preparing ahead of time, and staying true to that message?

It's an interesting question because my message has morphed over the years, and your business is going to morph. You're going to start with your message that works now, and all of a sudden you're going to do a speech on something else, and it hits it out of the park. You think, "What? That wasn't where I was going." That's okay. Let your audience tell you what messages are resonating with them. That's your research so take cues from that. Do a lot of practice speeches because some will bomb. Ask yourself, why did that bomb? Was it the message, the delivery, the workshop setting?

How has your message morphed?

Mine has evolved into what companies have called soft skills. I call them essential skills, because it's about confidence. You cannot gain more confidence if you're listening to the voice of self-doubt in your head. You just can't do it, and you can do mantras up the wazoo, but there's no way you're going to gain more confidence if you're listening to self-doubt. So, those are my messages. We have to communicate effectively. It's an essential skill and every leader needs that. The topic resonates with me, but I'm not sure it was particularly strategic in my case. I think it was more like the messages chose me because as that phrase is, you teach what you need to learn most. Back when I started, I needed the confidence. I needed to learn communication. It has morphed and evolved, and the response that I've gotten from my clients and from my audiences is that yes, this is exactly what we need to be talking about because nobody talks about this stuff in the way that I do it, right?

You've been successful at building a business that has several different revenue sources with different audiences and niches. How do you manage that?

I have been in business for myself for almost 25 years, and you learn a lot of things. I'm into professional development, so it always fascinated me how people could create massive businesses, and they're just one person. I thought, "That's it," because there are only so many hours in the day, and I can only be so many places at once, right? I thought, "You know, this is what I need to do but I have to do it in a way that is authentic, and that aligns with my values and my vision." I resonate with the television shows that I've been on here in the Twin Cities.

Their audiences are more for stay-at-home moms, and people who work different shifts, and they're looking for some life coaching, some work-life balance. I love that. I love to do video. The shows that I've been on have sets where you feel like you're sitting in somebody's living room. People would see me and go to my website, and I'd get clients from that.

How did you build up each area of your business?

The speaking came from coaching. I do leadership coaching and women's retreats. That came from a love of traveling, and a love of getting this message out, and they all tie together. There is a theme throughout everything that I do, and it's all about self-confidence, self-doubt, communication, and work-life integration. My tagline is, "Wisdom and Worthiness at Work." That means, at work, where you go to work every day and your career, and it also means 'at work inside of you'. Because creating new programs all the time is exhausting, you want to really hone your message. Then determine how many ways you can get it out to the world in a non-salesy, authentic way. I have found it is speaking, coaching, women's retreats. Those are my hot spots.

I've seen you do video and some social media, how would you recommend others approach getting into that?

Great question. Entrepreneurs, we're so funny. We do this "ready, set, ready, set, ready, set." We think we have to take all of these online courses. Then I've got to take a course on how to do webinars. Then I have to take a course on how to build a six-figure business doing an online course. And before we have written word one of any kind of a speech, we have invested thousands of dollars. I would say start small. If you like video, great. Be a ham. Get your smartphone out with a selfie stick and start doing some video. You're just going into your Toastmasters meeting. Isn't this exciting? Blah, blah, blah. Video creates buzz. Get a YouTube channel for sure, but remember to clarify your message. What are you going to do? Because video lasts forever.

What if I'm someone who's not comfortable speaking virtually?

If speaking online is not your thing, then think about how you can rewire your thoughts, because there's some fear there. What would you say if you were having coffee with someone? Do a Facebook Live for ten minutes, and pretend you're having coffee with someone. Here's the approach you want to take. Hey, how are you, Facebook? It's so benign, and people will either be on it or not. Social media can be such a black hole, but just do it for the practice of being in front of a camera and in front of an audience. This is the neat thing, we get to practice. Every time I do any kind of a speech, I'm thinking it is paid rehearsal one more time. I'm always honing. I never want to arrive at this place of, well, I'm perfect now. That's never going to happen for me. I always want the experience to be stellar for my audience, so don't get so hung up on having to be on Instagram, Twitter, and Facebook, and LinkedIn, because those are very different animals, and very different audiences, so know your audience.

It gets overwhelming.

No one has time for all of the stuff, unless you're twenty-something and in college, truly. If you were born in that generation where your thumbs are your main communicating tools, that's a whole different thing then someone that's in their forties, fifties, or sixties. You have to know who your audience is. There are so many layers to all this stuff, but I would say just start with a selfie thing, and just see. It doesn't have to be complicated. Start with five minutes on Facebook Live.

Yes, and a YouTube channel's free, you can use your phone, and in so many of the videos today, the style is natural and in the moment. It doesn't have to be a beautiful Apple background.

Here's the thing. Those are more interesting than polished and beautiful, and will grab more viewers. What's this guy doing walking down the street? Click. Those get likes but when you're first starting out, don't try to be a Michael Hyatt, because you're not. They have teams. They have crews. They have film people. These people make millions of dollars. We always try to run before we learn to crawl, and we have to pull it back. Just start by crawling and be okay with that.

What do you do right before you go out to speak? Is there something that you do to center yourself or get prepared?

I do two things. First, I go within, because I am a very spiritual person. I know that I am connected to my source, and I ask for my source to be with me in this next time frame, whether it's 45 minutes, or 90 minutes, so that I bring the message to this audience in a way that they can hear it, in a way that is entertaining to them, and that will impact their lives. It's about them. Let me be the vehicle for this message so that they hear it in the way that they need to hear it today. Second, The Wonder Woman pose. I learned that from Amy Cuddy, and I just loved her TED Talk. People look at me, like, "What is this woman doing?" Because I'm standing there with my hands on my hips in my Wonder Woman pose, chest out, going, "Dang. I own this room, sister. You have got this. You are gonna go and rock their world. They will not know what hit them. They will want more." I am standing in it for a good two minutes, which seems like an eternity when people are walking by you going, "What the what?" So, I do my Wonder Woman, and then I hit it.

Barbara, thinking back, if you knew then what you know now, what would you have done differently?

If I could turn back time, here's what I would do. I would understand that this is a long process. It's a journey, and it's a long and winding road that is fascinating and fun. It has highs. It has lows, and all of it is fabulous material to be used in my next speech. It's all about the experience of life. Don't rush it. Don't wish that you're going to be over there, because the juice is from where you are right now to getting to that point. Be exactly where you are, and be present with everything you're experiencing, the good stuff, and the stuff that didn't work. Use it to enhance what you're doing rather than to beat yourself up.

Golden nuggets.

Just enjoy that moment, because it is so much fun. Before I decide whether I'm going to speak, I talk to the person that's doing the hiring, and my barometer is, if I have goosebumps during that conversation, I do it. If I think it's going to be fun, I do it. If I don't have that, if nothing is resonating, if this doesn't sound like my group, I don't do it. I refer them to somebody else.

That's interesting, and it's a great barometer.

Yeah. I won't do stuff just for money.

Barbara, you've given us so many great tips and nuggets. Thank you for taking time to do this.

Thank you, Maria. I love what you do for your clients. You are amazing. Thanks so much for having me as part of this book. I love what you do, and I love how you empower fellow speakers, so thank you.

KEY TAKEAWAYS

- Give them three takeaways.
- Stories are like a little mini-theater. You want to draw them in.
- Detach from worrying if they are going to love you or not.
- Do a lot of practice speeches because some will bomb.
- Let your audience tell you what messages are resonating with them.

ABOUT BARBARA CHURCHILL

Barbara is the creator of *Live It Real* Leadership Coaching Program, and she combines her leadership and communication expertise, which can be found on a college campus, at a sales conference, or in the boardroom, sharing her messages of personal development and empowerment. Barbara continues to be invited by Fortune 100 companies to lead sessions on self-confidence and leadership, and she's a frequent television guest in the Twin Cities market. She believes that everyone should have permission to be themselves, and she leads leadership retreats that help women unplug from the frenzy of daily life to reconnect with their vision and passion.

CONTACT

You can learn more about Barbara on her website, at www.barbarachurchill.com where she has a free video series available. You can also email at barbara@barbarachurchill.com. Barbara also welcomes your call at 952-200-5643. She is available on regular social media channels.

CHAPTER 20:
ANNIE MEEHAN

"When you look people in the eye, and speak their name, truth and hope into them, it will change their lives."
-Annie Meehan

Annie Meehan is an award-winning speaker, author, and life coach out of Minneapolis, Minnesota. After starting her career in corporate America, she's now seen as the powerful, successful motivational speaker with heart and determination that awakens her audience to action. Annie is a member of the National Speakers Association, a graduate of their apprentice program, and a certified coach. She has been a guest on *Oprah* and *Twin Cities Live*, a local celebrity show, and today she is speaking across the country and internationally.

Welcome, Annie. Thank you so much for being here!

Absolutely. Excited to work with you, Maria.

Let's start from the beginning. How did you know you wanted to be a speaker?

I started in my church with youth groups, women's ministry and women's retreats. Ten years ago, my husband and I bought a gym, so companies started asking me to come in and speak about wellness. They would ask, "Can you teach us how to get fit in five minutes?" "Can you teach us how to be healthy?" In addition to physical health, I also speak about mental and emotional health. So, I started as a faith speaker and moved into wellness.

From there, how did you move into public speaking?

After two years of owning the gym, I was interviewed for a TV commercial. The woman interviewing me said, "There's more to your story, Annie Meehan. Tell me what your big dream is. I said, "Oh, that's easy. I'm the next Tony Robbins." I told her I've always visualized myself on a stage in front of tens of thousands of people, inspiring people to overcome whatever obstacle they experience in life. She said, "You have to talk to someone from the National Speakers Association." After that, I signed up for their Academy Program and started creating my own programs, and my speaking grew. I talked about goal setting, the power of our words, and choosing change. Today, I have about nine topics, which I know some people recommend against. But for me, my talks come from my life experiences, so I speak on many things.

What was it like the first time you got a big speaking gig?

Speaking is very natural for me. I don't get nervous at all, whether it's four people or 4,000 people. I never feel nervous speaking in front of an audience. What I do feel nervous about is sharing vulnerable stories. That's still hard for me. In March, it will be four years since I hung my hat on the wall and said, "This is what I do." And though it can still be difficult, I know I connect more with the audience when I speak from my heart about what I've had to overcome to find strength and success. I find speaking exhilarating. I work with other speakers, and run a mastermind group once a month. Recently one of the speakers said, "Do you know what the real standing ovation is? It's when we leave the room, and a week or month later we get an email or a handwritten note saying, 'You changed my life, you make me want to be a better person, or you gave me a new perspective.'"

You talked about the emotional part being the most difficult part. How do you open yourself up and bring in that deep emotion at the right level?

I think more than anything, Maria, we need to be healed. People first need to heal from those painful things in life to be able to talk about them. Taking a risk in sharing about a death, tragedy, hardship or excruciating pain in your life will connect you with at least one person in your audience. When I do, I sometimes still feel very emotional. Especially since I've been talking more about my mom in the past year, and that longing for what I didn't have. Sometimes a tear comes to my eyes, and I say, "I just want you to know this is still really hard for me." But, people will come up to you because you've been authentic with them and shared your truth. It will make them more comfortable to share their story and their truth. I find it also leads to people wanting to refer me. So, I mentally prepare by saying the gift is worth the risk of being vulnerable, knowing the audience will gain from my presentation. That's how I get through it.

What would you suggest people do when they tell stories, whether painful or funny, that make people want to refer you afterwards?

Absolutely. I've heard it over and over, "facts tell and stories sell." What I'm trying to sell more than anything is the concept that there's a silver lining in everything in life. I think most people get stuck on the tragedy, and they lose sight that there's a silver lining. There is no situation that a person can share with me that doesn't have some goodness I can help them see. I know that stories sell a message, and people remember stories more than facts. Also, stories connect me with the audience. One thing I often say in a presentation is, "Let me just be honest, I'm messy. I'm going to screw something up today. If you have high expectations of me, I hope you lower them now. I've lowered mine." I think stories help paint that picture.

How do you come up with new stories?

When I'm working, other speakers say, "How do you have so many stories?" I say, "I get 12 new stories every day because I watch things and pay attention whether I'm at a restaurant, a coffee shop, or the gas station. I see what other people don't notice." I'm always looking for the story behind the story. We judge people in seven seconds. We think, "Hmm. She's got it all together." "Ooh, she's falling apart, she's messy," or "Oh, he looks smart." But what if, instead of judging, we wondered? What if we wondered, "Hmm. I wonder why she dresses up? Does she love clothes? Did her mom teach her that? What might she be covering up?" Wondering instead of judging changes our perspective on life.

What's a good way to tell stories?

I like making one point, then telling one story about you, one story about the audience. That way you have a nice flow of connecting and sharing pieces, but it's not too much about you or them. Also, don't give a list of experiences. Give one example of your own personal experience, and one example of a potential personal experience for them. But, use stories, not lists, to teach.

What's a common theme behind your stories?

I'm not a perfectionist. I like to ask, "How does a perfectionist go to bed?" And I love how different audiences answer that question. Most of them will say things like, "The exact same way every night." And I say, "No, no. They go to bed every night disappointed." On the other hand, how does a person that accepts their messiness go to bed? "Hey, I only screwed up five things today, not ten." In my stories, I talk about the fact that I'm not perfect. When I recognized that I will never be perfect, but I'm still good, it was really a powerful point in my life. I could say, "There is goodness and strength in me, I have some things I'm really good at. I have a whole bunch of things I'm not good at." I need to surround myself with people who are good with

Annie Meehan

attention to detail and organization. I like to create and visualize the picture. With stories, I get people to laugh at me and with me about the silly things I do. I teach self-acceptance, and how to take a breath. You know what? You don't have to act like you have it all together.

It's about engaging with your audience.

Absolutely. It must be conversational. Once you say you're a little messy, it lets the audience breathe. It lets you breathe. You can be more real with them. And they receive you as another human being, rather than this perfect person. One of my mentors said, " Annie, when you're done speaking and you leave that room, give them the gift of helping them better their lives. Share the parts of your story that can be applied to their life." That is so helpful to me every time I speak. I think, "How can I give them some hope and encouragement in whatever they're walking through?" Because if I feel I'm always incapable, then I'm never going to write the book or give the talk. But, if I decide that's *not* the truth, then I can rewrite a new ending to the story. It's about connecting with the audience and leaving them with a gift of a hope.

You mentioned you have nine different topics. What do they have in common?

At the end of the day, all my topics overlap in asking, "How do I become the exception?" Not the expert. I'm not an expert on anything, but I will go out of my way to be kind and generous to people. I will give more than I receive to people who are struggling, just like I struggled. If I can be a little bit of hope, love, and encouragement then I've made a difference.

Why do you think your talks are so life-changing for people?

I draw from my life. I know what it's like to go without, and that experience has allowed me to experience joy. I count my blessings knowing that not everyone has food on the table or a bed to sleep in, let alone a career that they love. I get to make a positive impact on the world. I realize it's a privilege to walk into a room and bring joy and light. Now, if you ask my family if I live these out perfectly, they would tell you, "No." But I try.

What advice do you have for others who want to share their journey?

When I meet people that want to speak, I always say, "Why does it matter what you have to say? What difference does it make for the audience? They don't care about your divorce or your traumatic situation." I tell them, "Doesn't matter. Doesn't matter," and I make them mad. Until they can convince me that that they can teach others through their story, then it doesn't matter. Because it's never about us.

What's the first thing you would say to someone starting out as a speaker?

Practice. Speak all the time. Create events. Invite your friends and families. The more you do it, the better you get. Don't just jump in and try to be a professional speaker. Start by practicing speaking all the time. You can try out Toastmasters, but just start practicing. Just like anything in life, practice, practice, practice. Just get out there. Have great success. Never let anyone tell you that you can't achieve your dreams.

How do you prepare? Do you have a process to come up with your material?

I just want to remind you, I'm super messy. Every time is unique and different. People call me and ask me to create a talk for them on a certain topic. They've seen my videos on YouTube and they'll say, "Hey, I love your style and your personality. Here is our topic." If I can't refer it out, then I create a topic. I tend to use my phone and notes, or just click the voice recorder and start talking. Then I email it to myself, read it, and rewrite it. I'm writing a lot. I love interactive presentations where I'm doing some exercises with them. But when doing a keynote, I'm not able to be as interactive. This year, my hope is to really hone people in on choosing to be the exception along with the seven steps, which is based on my book. In a one-hour keynote, I can do three of the seven steps.

You're great at winging it, but, has there ever been something that threw you off? What was the worst experience you've had, and how did you recover?

Two years ago, I was speaking at the IDS Tower in downtown Minneapolis and I got a phone call from a fellow speaker. She said, "Hey, I'm at a conference, and your picture is on the sign. It says you're speaking in 20 minutes. Where are you?" I said, "Oh my gosh!" I was in Minneapolis, and the conference was in White Bear Lake, which is not even close! They had never confirmed or sent back my contract or invoice, so I had nothing on my calendar. I raced over there, but I missed the morning presentation. I didn't have my PowerPoint slides or my handouts. The other sessions ended up being okay, and I received some good feedback, but I didn't feel good about the presentation. I still got paid for it, so that was nice. But, that was probably my worst situation.

What advice would you give someone who is in a similar kind of situation?

Own it. Apologize. Move forward. I heard a speaker the other day, and he said, "There are only two speeches in the world," and I was thinking, "Really? There's got to be more than two speeches, I have nine, come on." And he said, "The one you gave, and the one you wish you gave." Don't get caught up worrying about what you might have done wrong. Accept it and carry on.

Do you use evaluations?

I had a friend tell me he throws away all course evaluations. I don't do that personally, because I enjoy reading them. If you do ask people for feedback, don't read too much into it. There is always someone that says the room was too cold, the room was too hot, you talk too fast, you talk too slow. When you get negative feedback, don't be too hard on yourself. My evaluations say, please tell me one thing you loved or learned today, so it focuses their attention on what did work for them. I don't take myself or the feedback too seriously.

Thinking back, if you knew then what you know now, what would you have done differently when you were just starting out?

I was originally too cautious. I'm blessed to have had an amazing mentor. He said, "Annie, you have this amazing story but you stayed at this really safe level. I know what he was saying, and I do share more than I have in the past, but I still am cautious. If I could encourage new speakers, I would say speak the truth of what you've overcome, what you've walked through. Even though it might be hard, risk more.

If you could be remembered for one thing, what would it be?

It really is to be the exception. I think a lot of my story is about resilience and breaking the cycle. It's about standing up for and doing the right thing. But I want it to be more than just, "She broke the cycle and didn't repeat it." I want it to be that I gave more than I received. "Annie looked people in the eye and believed in them the way others believed in her along the way."

Thank you so much for sharing today. Is there any last advice you want to give to speakers who might be starting out or building a business?

First, never give up. It's going to be hard, but don't give up. Second, don't quit your day job until you can afford to. Keep pursuing this, in the evenings and on the weekends. Speak whenever anyone will let you speak. Speak for free or for fee. Even if you make a difference in one person's life, it's worth it. Third, words are powerful, so use them for good. People need positive, encouraging words in their life. When you look someone in the eye and speak their name, and you speak truth and hope into them, it will change their whole life. Never underestimate the power of your words. Use them for good. I wish you all the best, and if I can help you in any way on your journey, please feel free to ask.

Thank you for being the exception, Annie! This was fun.

Awesome, thanks Maria.

KEY TAKEAWAYS:

- Practice, Practice, Practice.
- If you make a difference in one person's life, it's worth it.
- Stories are all around you if you pay attention.
- It's going to be hard, but never give up.
- Don't take yourself or the feedback too seriously.

ABOUT ANNIE MEEHAN:

Annie journeyed through life as the middle child of seven, raised by a single mom, and has many stories and life lessons to share. She draws from her personal and professional expertise to deliver dynamic and interactive presentations that inspire her audience. She is the award-winner author of *Be the Exception; Be the Exception Bible Study; and Paths, Detours, and Possibilities.*

CONTACT:

You can reach Annie on her website at www.anniemeehan.com, where she has a blog and a weekly "Choose Letter" available. Annie can also be found on YouTube with her Vlog, where she provides helpful videos and talks. She is active on social media.

YOUR NEXT MOVE

Thank you for joining me on this amazing journey. In these pages, you've seen 20 master speakers openly share their beginnings, their lessons learned, and their painstaking journeys to success. Connecting with these individuals has been both humbling and inspiring. My hope is that you've been equally inspired to take action and share your voice at a higher level, in whatever form that might take.

There is no magic pill. Even the greatest speakers in the world start out at square one. Know that showing up requires work, but the rewards are immense. The good news is that speaking skills can be learned, so you can take this as far as you're willing to go.

As an easy first step, be sure to access the Free Speaker Bonus Page. Simply go to www.MariaLynnJohnson.com/Bonus to access the gifts listed below.

1) A practical QUICK START SPEAKING GUIDE with steps to get ready and booked

2) A powerful ANTHOLOGY OF QUOTES from the speakers

3) Exclusive access to my weekly SPEAKER NOTES, which include relevant, cutting edge tips and techniques on the concepts covered in the book. You'll also receive the inside scoop on what's happening with me and the speakers in this book.

At this point, you may be ready to dive in and asking, "Now what?" For those of you who are ready to take it deeper and want guidance on putting what you've learned into action, I invite you to reach out. I offer free Speaking Strategy Sessions for us to pull up our sleeves and see where you're at, where you want to be, and the best way to get there. You can sign up here: www.MariaLynnJohnson.com/About.

Wherever you're at, know that taking imperfect action is always your next move. Many of the speakers talked about wishing they hadn't waited so long to start. Now's the time. Begin by committing to one action you will take immediately after reading this. Stick with it and maybe someday I'll be interviewing YOU.